LOST NAPA VALLEY

LOST NAPA VALLEY

LAUREN COODLEY

THE History PRESS

Published by The History Press
Charleston, SC
www.historypress.com

Front cover: Napa State Hospital, mid-1940s. Courtesy of Napa County Historical Society.
Back cover: Fox Theatre, 1920s. Courtesy of Tom Malloy; *inset*: steamboat on Napa River. Postcard courtesy of Mr. M.

First published 2021

Manufactured in the United States

ISBN 9781467147644

Library of Congress Control Number: 2020948648

Dedicated to Cathy Mathews, descendant of Jose Mateus, whose hilarious memories have enabled me to understand lost Napa, and to Professor Doug Dibble, my brilliant colleague and collaborator at Napa College who helped me introduce hundreds of students to real history.

CONTENTS

Contents

ACKNOWLEDGEMENTS

My thanks to the many contributors to this book, who generously shared their insights, research and poetry: Cathy Mathews, Marlene Wilson Hurley, Michael Amen, Ellwin Jobe, Pat Stanley, Harvey Schwartz, Sudie Pollock, Roxann Gracia, Michael McFee, Kevin Courtney, Paula Amen Judah, Tucker Catlin, Brent McKee, Patricia Prestina, Doug Murray, Ray Guadagni, Scott Sedgley, Tanya Barry, Kathy Bazolli, Maurice Marciano, Dina Dwyer, Stephanie Grohs, Tony Norris, Amber Manfree, Timothy Murphy, Barry Nelson, Jeff Johnson, Deborah Fortune, Ron Kyle, Peggy Aaron, Deanna Krueckemeier Fogerty, Judy Harrison, Terry Longoria, Ray Guadagni, Carolyn Younger, Patty Alexander, Wendy Beltrami, Mary Campbell, Jeff Doran and Leonore Wilson—as well as those who contributed anecdote and memory to previous research, mentioned in the works cited.

I was ably assisted in organizing this material firstly by Ilenna Brown and then by Adaira Grohs, whose steady hand helped me bring it to completion amid illness, a pandemic and wildfires. The book would not be possible without their efforts. Laurie Krill and Rick Delaney have been outstanding and compassionate editors from the very beginning of *Lost Napa Valley*. The Napa County Historical Society has been most generous with access to photographs and archives. I thank Napa Valley Marketplace magazine, which has published my research for over a decade. Patty Alexander encouraged me to create this volume and introduced me to Greta Ericson through her marvelous children's book. The *Napa Register* archives are an outstanding repository of local stories, and I salute the reporters who generously shared their work here. To the extended family who kept me going with broth—Ines Donnelly, Sherry Melton, Danielle Alexander, Angeles Iricuta and Anita Catlin: thank you for nourishing me. To my children and grandsons: may what is lost be replaced by what is found.

PREFACE

Before all the homes and farms and stores and factories, before all the swimming pools and bowling alleys and skating rinks, there were thousands of years of indigenous life in the Napa Valley. Photography was developed just after the gold rush, but nobody photographed the forced removal of the indigenous people from the valley. Known to themselves as the "Water Going Out Place People," because of the importance of the river and the tides to their life, these peoples left few dwellings on the land, which furnished the plants and animals central to their survival.

Thus the story of lost Napa must begin with the partial disappearance of these people, through removal to Sonoma and Lake Counties, through bounties paid for the murder of individual "Indians," through European diseases and through marriage to the first group of colonizers, the Spanish. Tribes survive throughout Northern California who are the descendants of these Napa Valley residents.

History does not begin with the missions, yet the last mission built in California, in Sonoma in 1820, marks the beginning of the period of Mexican rule, which lasted a scant twenty years. Mariano Vallejo led troops to pacify and corral indigenous residents of this region. Having captured the land, he then gave out huge tracts, called land grants, to a favored handful of his men. Among these were George Yount, Julian Pope and Cayetano Juarez, men who lived the Californio lifestyle of cattle raising and citrus growing, housing huge families and an indigenous workforce.

With the discovery of gold, settlers from the Midwest and East Coast of America rushed into California. Vallejo himself was arrested. A war was fought, and won, for control of California; one year after the gold rush began, it became a state. This book begins with the first farms granted to Californio landholders before the war. Chinese men had come to the gold coast as miners and were soon dispersed to work in the tanneries and orchards of the valley. Their settlements in St. Helena and Napa form part of the beginning of the twentieth-century story. Italian immigrants found the climate very similar to that of their country and quickly became a sizable part of the Napa population.

A part of downtown once named for Juarez and Vallejo was home to the Chinese; Juarez sold parts of his land grant to build an asylum and to create a neighborhood later known as Little Italy. Today, those neighborhoods are known to tourists as "downtown" and "the oxbow." Two different railroads traversed the narrow valley, allowing for the development of factories along the tracks and the river, carrying goods and people for generations. Now those tracks carry the Wine Train, a luxury excursion for tourists and locals who can afford to ride.

This book traces the trajectory of the twentieth century, when factories began to close along with those across the country. Small businesses faltered; most in Napa lost out to the big-box stores that covered a strip of flood zone once the floodplain was reclaimed and rezoned after the 1986 Great Flood. With the triumph of the viticulture and tourist economies, housing and commercial real estate became unaffordable for most Napa Valley residents.

Against that backdrop, children trooped to school and parents to jobs. People found recreation where they could. This book traces those memories and attempts to lay down markers of places that live no more. For every location included, there are a hundred untold stories. I hope this book, and what was unavoidably omitted, will encourage readers to begin recording that which must be remembered.

All excerpted poems, except those otherwise indicated, were written by the author.

1
WHERE WE FARMED

Farmyards were stages for concerts of sound. Doors squeaked and slammed. Boards were sawed and hammered. Boots made great sucking sounds when pulled out of the mud. Sweeping was a snare drum, raising clouds of dust. Rocks were broken and foundations were poured. Restive horses whinnied and neighed, cows bellowed...all the while the clinking and sucking pump filled buckets with splashing and swirling water.

—Joseph Amato, *Rethinking Home*

Over millions of years, the tectonic collision of the Pacific Oceanic and North American continental plates created the landform of the Napa Valley. Explosive volcanic activity created a series of layers consisting of oceanic crust, marine sediment, volcanic rock and, at the surface, Napa River soil deposits. This unique mixture of inorganic and organic soils, combined with environmental influences, created one of the most fertile valleys in the world, paving the way for plant, animal and human populations. Glass Mountain, located on the eastern side of the valley between Calistoga and St. Helena, was formed by a flow of molten glass that poured out of the earth's interior. The volcanic glass, known as obsidian, was used by the indigenous population to form highly specialized tools, such as spearpoints, scrapers and projectile points. Through the geologic process of sedimentation, folding, faulting, uplifting and erosion, the base of today's rich soils was formed. It is the fertility of these soils that has made the Napa Valley famous agriculturally.

California Black Oak. *Courtesy of Lauren Coodley.*

The original inhabitants of Napa's valley drew nourishment from the plants that were growing here, via the hunter-gatherer lifestyle characteristic of all original peoples. Because the plant world was sacred and central to their lives, indigenous residents developed many methods of plant cultivation and care. They pruned, weeded and aerated the soil, carefully taking only the plants they needed. When they gathered seeds for pinole, they cast a few handfuls back to the ground to ensure a yield the following season. They pruned shrubs almost to the ground, stimulating regrowth of the long, straight, slender branches needed for tool- and basket-making, and they periodically burned the landscape to control underbrush and acorn and bulb growth.

To add to their food stores, the entire tribe walked the one-hundred-mile round trip once a year to the Sonoma coast, where they gathered abalone, clams, crabs, mussels, dry seaweed and salt. In the spring and summer, they walked up to Clear Lake, where they caught and dried fish and carried them home. The paths of these peoples were the origins of today's Highway 29, Silverado Trail and Monticello Road.

RANCHO OF CAYETANO JUAREZ, EAST NAPA

In 1821, the lives of indigenous peoples changed dramatically when the Mexican government built what would be the last mission in Sonoma. In order to obtain this land, General Mariano Vallejo led the Mexican army as it dislocated the indigenous residents and apportioned the hills and the valley east of Sonoma to his friends, a group who called themselves Californios. In 1835, Vallejo persuaded Sam Yeto, a leader of the Suisun tribe, to assist him in the final defeat of the Mey'ankmah, and he gave Yeto the title "Chief of the Unconverted Indians." After they combined forces and defeated the Mey'ankmah in the Suscol area, Vallejo awarded Yeto the protection of a mounted honor guard dressed in full military uniform.

Under Mexican rule, cattle ranching and wheat growing in California began, offering economic opportunities to Californios while indigenous and landless Mexican peoples remained in a permanent position of servitude on the ranchos. Californios prospered, growing citrus fruit, corn, beans, barley, peas, mission grapes, nuts and wheat. They threshed wheat by piling it inside an enclosure and driving wild mustangs around and around at high speeds until the wheat was pulverized. Workers then repeatedly lifted and tossed the mass with forks until the wind blew away the straw and chaff, leaving the grain, which was washed, dried and made ready for milling.

Cattle ranching came to Napa in the 1830s, when Nasario Berryessa brought five thousand head of cattle to the area, which he ran between Berryessa and Capay Valleys. Landless Mexicans, along with indigenous workers, ran the *matanzas* (cattle slaughters) for the landholding families. They left the carcasses for the wild animals. These men skinned the cattle, melted the fat or tallow into skin bags and transported the goods to trading ships. The landholding Californios profited from the flourishing fur and tallow trade. Russians from Alaska brought indigenous Aleuts to hunt sea otter, and the Californios sold furs to New England maritime merchants.

Cayetano Juarez was a sergeant in the Mexican army who helped General Vallejo found the Sonoma Presidio. But in 1837, when Mexico refused to pay its soldiers, Sergeant Juarez organized troops to ride to Monterey and demand payment. Sam Yeto (Chief Solano), still loyal to Vallejo, reported the desertion. Vallejo confronted the soldiers as they were mounting their horses, reminding them of the law of capital punishment for desertion. Everyone but Juarez returned to duty, so Juarez left alone and swam across the Carquinez Straits with his horse. Just short of Monterey, he was captured and sentenced to be shot. Vallejo intervened and offered him a land grant in Napa. In return, Juarez had to allow Vallejo to direct his personal life, and so Vallejo chose his wife.

Juarez built his first adobe on the Tulocay Rancho, which covered more than 8,800 acres. In 1845 and 1874, he built more houses to accommodate his growing family, and once a year, his family held a rodeo. His children attended school in Sonoma and spent weekends in General Vallejo's home. At the Tulocay Rancho, over four hundred indigenous people raised cattle and crops. Juarez's wife, Maria, performed manual labor and used local herbs for healing, cooking and cleaning. Her children grew up speaking Spanish and Uluca, a Patwin dialect.

One of the Juarez daughters spent many hours with the indigenous women at the rancho, exchanging information regarding menstruation and childbirth. Domitila Juarez Metcalf, who grew up on the Tulocay Rancho, remembered a cholera epidemic in which Indian servants in the house "would die before their very eyes, and the men in the fields dropped in their tracks." According to her granddaughter Vivian Juarez Rose, Metcalf told an interviewer in 1920 that the Spanish did not contract the disease. While the Californio men were away in Sonoma, their wives managed on their own in Napa. These Californianas were trained in horseback riding and the use of small arms; they did not go out without their weapons for fear of indigenous attack. In addition to running the ranchos, the women were expected to produce large families: Maria Juarez had eleven children at Rancho Tulocay; Mariano Vallejo's wife had sixteen. The pressure on Californianas to reproduce was so strong that when one of the Juarez daughters, Agnes, entered the Dominican convent, her father was angry enough to threaten her with violence.

In 1848, at the end of the Mexican-American War, America gained much of the territory that was once Mexico, and Californio rights to land ownership ended. American settlers from all parts of the country moved in to claim the land or to buy it. That year, Smith Brown bought land from Cayetano Juarez on which to grow wheat. While once indigenous people had harvested wheat at the missions using wild horses, now it could be done with mechanical machinery pulled by domestic horses.

Left: Cayetano Juarez and his son. Juarez donated the land for Tulocay Cemetery in 1858; the Juarez family burial site is located there. *Courtesy of Napa County Historical Society.*

Below: Last residence of Cayetano and Maria Juarez, Silverado Trail, 1874. *Courtesy of Napa County Historical Society.*

Prior to 1861, the land east of the new town of Napa was a vast cattle range. The severe winter that year was followed by a great drought in the valley in 1863–65. Due to a lack of grain to feed their cattle, ranchers were forced to sell their recently built-up herds. When the drought years ended, wheat was replanted and again became the valley's major crop. Cattle ranching and the associated hide and tallow trade were never restored to their former economic importance.

On September 30, 1865, Reverend John Jamison Moore, founding pastor of the first AME Zion Church in California, visited members of the African American community in Napa Valley, including community leader Edward Hatton. Moore's observations were printed in the *Elevator*, a weekly San Francisco newspaper established in 1865: "Our greatest pleasure was to find in the Valley, within a radius of ten miles from Napa, so many industrious colored farmers." Among these were Isabel Holman, who cultivated one hundred acres with nine head of stock and raised 1,500 sacks of wheat, and Jacob Sinclair, who had two hundred acres with forty head of stock and 2,500 sacks of wheat and barley.

STODDARD'S MILL, NAPA

In 1873, C.A. Menefee commented, "There are fewer localities in the world where wheat will grow better than in the Napa Valley…nearly the whole of the land in the valley is adapted to all kinds of cereals." After wheat was cut, it was piled in an open area and either baled for feed or winnowed, by which the grain was separated from the chaff. William Stoddard traveled west by wagon train from Michigan and settled in Napa in 1880. With his sons he soon established a prosperous grain and feed business that became one of the largest in the region, milling barley and corn. Farmers piled the grain onto horse-drawn wagons and drove it to mills like Stoddard's. Well over 10 percent of all grain in the United States came from Napa County. Pressure to diversify was partly caused by a declining price on wheat brought about by overproduction.

THOMPSON BROTHERS ORCHARDS, SUSCOL CREEK

Former gold miner William Thompson traded lumber with Mariano Vallejo. In return for the lumber, Vallejo gave Thompson a parcel of his

Workers at Stoddard Milling, established in 1880. *Courtesy of Napa County Historical Society.*

Postcard, "Orchard in Bloom." *Courtesy of Mr. M.*

land, and Thompson purchased an additional three hundred acres. In 1852, Thompson's brother Simpson suggested planting a fruit orchard. Gold seekers were sick of their monotonous diet of beef and grain, and some were able and willing to pay high prices for fresh fruit.

Thompson and his brother ordered saplings to be delivered by boat from the East Coast. They planted the first peach and apple trees near Suscol Creek, which they diverted and channeled for irrigation. By 1860, Thompson's Gardens were known all over the West, with 150,000 fruit trees thriving. In 1869, when the first transcontinental railroad roared to life, Napa's fruit production exploded. Napa offered the ideal climate and available land even for people who didn't have a lot of money.

OAK KNOLL

The Oak Knoll area was originally part of Salvador Vallejo's Rancho de Napa land grant. It took first prize in the 1856 competition for "Best Farm in California." Joseph Osborne bought a spread of land north of Napa, planted orchards and a vineyard and named the plantation Oak Knoll.

The first execution in Napa County was of Charles Britton, a laborer at Oak Knoll. In 1863, when he couldn't cash his paycheck, he took a steamer to San Francisco and bought a revolver. He killed Joseph Osborne. He was hanged in 1863 at the Napa Courthouse. Osborne's survivors sold Oak Knoll to R.B. Woodward.

The R.B. Woodward estate at Oak Knoll, 1870. *Courtesy of Napa County Historical Society.*

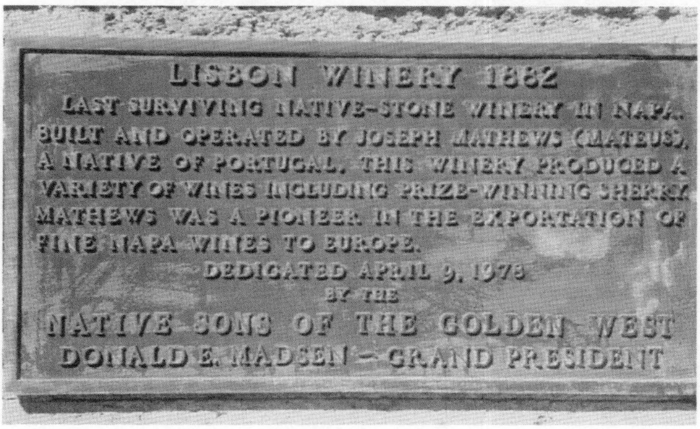

Top: The Jarvis Conservatory, dedicated to the Zarzuela of Iberia, Jose Mateus's birthplace. *Courtesy of Cathy Mathews.*

Bottom: Plaque outside Lisbon Winery. *Courtesy of Cathy Mathews.*

Woodward hired Jose Mateus, who had emigrated from Portugal, as his wine and brandy maker. Mateus left Oak Knoll in 1877 to establish his own winery in Napa City. In 1882, Mateus built the Lisbon Winery at 1720 Brown Street, known for its sherry. Mateus constructed the building from native stone quarried east of the city. An accomplished stonemason, Mateus built the decorative arches of the doorways himself. By the end of the nineteenth century, he had lost the business in a gambling game in San Francisco. The structure has been converted to the Jarvis Conservatory.

VOLZ AND VINEY RANCHES, YOUNTVILLE

In 1881, Frederick and Mary Volz bought 188 acres one mile south of Yountville, between the Veterans Home and the Grigsby Ranch. They were able to keep the land for over eighty years, not selling it until 1972. Lois

View from Volz family ranch looking southeast, 1881. The Volz ranch was located between the Veterans Home–California and the Grigsby property. The Volz family was able to keep the ranch until 1972. *Courtesy of Phyllis Vallerga.*

Yountville resident Edward Van de Leur riding his horse on the Viney Ranch in 1936. *Courtesy of Lee Hart.*

Bauman Bishop and her sister Phyllis Bauman Vallerga are the descendants of the Volz family.

Many Yountville children learned early on to hunt game, drive tractors, shovel hay and ride horses. The Viney Ranch is located south of the St. Joan of Arc Catholic Church on Washington Street. According to John Callison:

> *Mr. Ghirardi was the last man in the valley to farm with mule teams. You could hear his mules all over town when they started braying…He plowed, disked, harrowed, planted, and harvested with his mules. He took the hay to his farm northwest of town and stored it in his barn. He also pruned and burned Bardessono's vineyard next to the school. He used a burn wagon after pruning the vines. It was quite a sight to see the wagon with flames shooting out and smoke billowing up moving around the vineyard. It never seems to bother his mules, however.*

NOBUJIRO NISHIZU, WHEELER RANCH, ST. HELENA

Clarence Iwao Nishizu was interviewed in 1982 about his immigrant father's experience working at a St. Helena vineyard. In 1902, Nobujiro Nishizu traveled from the village of Tachibana to San Francisco: "He went to work on a farm for a person by the name of Wheeler in Napa County, at a place called Zinfandel Lane, near the town of St. Helena. My uncle was there too. He worked for Mr. Wheeler who became rich by inventing and making cream of tartar."

By 1900, about two thousand Japanese immigrants already lived in San Francisco, while five hundred or so had found a home in Southern California. Japanese laborers began to be increasingly important to the success of California agriculture. Yet, like the Chinese before them, they were viewed with suspicion. The *Napa Daily Journal* of 1904 reveals that "the few citizens with the courage to oppose public opinion did so at some peril. The Wheeler family allowed a number of Japanese workers to live on their ranch on Zinfandel Lane. Threats were made, and it was feared that 'strong sentiment in certain corners' would result in violence."

The Wheeler family chose to ignore the pressure, and John Wheeler encouraged Mr. Nishizu to bring other neighbors and relatives to work on the farm. One of the casualties of the San Francisco earthquake in 1906 was John Wheeler's cream of tartar works, destroyed in the fires. Nishizu left St. Helena for Colorado, hoping to go into farming for himself. He ended

Two Japanese American men in front of the Napa train station. *Courtesy of the Department of Special Collections and University Archives, California State University Sacramento.*

up working as a sharecropper. In 1907, his relatives arranged for a young woman he had never met to travel to America to marry him. Clarence Nichizu was born to these parents in 1911.

In Napa County, by 1914, elected officials were warning voters of a disaster for California's grape and wine industry if Prohibition became law. J.H. Wheeler joined other small farmers to form the Napa County Viticulture Protective Agency. By 1916, Prohibition proponents from the Anti-Saloon League bought advertising on Napa's electric train cars. When the California Grape Protective Association condemned saloons, an outraged John Wheeler and other vintners withdrew from the association in protest. When Prohibition passed in 1920, Wheeler was prepared to go into the grape-juice business. But by 1923, he had changed his mind, ripped up his grapes and planted walnut trees.

Clarence Nichizu remembers his parents' pilgrimage back to St. Helena: "In 1927, during the summer vacation after my sophomore year in Anaheim High School, my family went to Yosemite and, afterwards, to Napa County to see Mr. Wheeler." The Southern Pacific Railroad provided passenger service to Napa until 1929, so the trio likely would have traveled up from Los Angeles on the train. The family found Mr. Wheeler at home, and they were pleased when he recognized Mr. Nishizu. Seventy years later, in 1991, when he was eighty years old, Clarence Nishizu and his wife, Helen, repeated the family pilgrimage, journeying one last time up valley: "We stopped at the old Wheeler house, which is over one hundred years old, and knocked at the door, but nobody was home. The stately mansion still stands like the day it was built with an ornate stone wall around the outside of the house."

The Nishizus wanted to find out what happened to Mr. Wheeler. They visited the St. Helena Grower's Foundation and spoke with the secretary, who recalled that her father had once worked for Wheeler. Raymond Vineyards bought the property in 1974 and operates a vineyard there.

ST. JOSEPH'S FARM, RUTHERFORD

George Yount's granddaughter Lizzie, who married San Francisco entrepreneur Thomas Lewis Rutherford, received one thousand acres of land as a wedding present from her grandfather in 1864. Just before the turn of the century, Lizzie Yount lost her estate due to debts and taxes, but she had managed to keep its one thousand acres intact for nearly thirty-five years. From that time, the Rutherford property was farmed, first in cattle and wheat, and later in vineyards, plus fruit and nut orchards.

The Roman Catholic Archdiocese of San Francisco purchased what was known as the "Rutherford tract" in 1902, five years after Lizzie had lost her property to a San Francisco bank. The archdiocese considered the site ideal for establishing a boys' school and farm training center to be named St. Joseph's Agricultural Institute. The school was thriving under the direction of Father Dennis O. Crowley. The rich and fertile site became a model agrarian estate dedicated to benefiting poor and homeless boys from San Francisco so that they could learn agricultural science and receive practical training. When Father Crowley first assumed stewardship of the school, he told a reporter:

> *It is the purpose to build a college in which can be taught theoretical and practical farming in all its branches including horticulture, viticulture, beekeeping and dairying. There is an excellent creamery now on the place...poultry will also be a lucrative industry...truck farming, especially the raising of vegetables, will also be a prominent feature. It has been considered that farming, the basis of all wealth, required no special training; all that was necessary was to go at it....Now it is recognized that farming requires just as much intelligence, to be successful, as any other calling. We believe that this farm, the first of its kind in the State, will give an impetus to agriculture.*

By 1908, the school was also planting mulberry trees for the raising of silkworms. This endeavor owed its inspiration to the efforts three decades earlier of San Francisco matron and suffragette Elise Wiehe Hittel, whose brother-in-law, historian John Hittel, was a Napa Valley landowner. The *Pacific Rural Press* reported:

> *Crowley has a lot of wide-awake boys in his charge, and they are to be kept busy with the worm feeding and spinning and can demonstrate what*

St. Joseph's Agriculture Institute, with school downstairs and the dormitory upstairs. *Courtesy of Napa County Historical Society.*

> *can be made out of it....If Father Crowley cannot make it work with his boys, the Silk Culture Society had better go to sleep again for a generation or until we have people who cannot make easy money in ways they like better than caterpillars.*

Mrs. Hittel was the first president of the Ladies Silk Culture Society of California. She had published a book on silk production, established a silk culture experimental station for girls in Piedmont, Alameda County, and became one of the first female members of the California Academy of Sciences. Hittel's Piedmont enterprise was the model for St. Joseph's silk production, which Mrs. D.J. Murphy, widow of San Francisco's former district attorney, organized for Father Crowley on Lizzie Yount's former homestead.

Meanwhile, Father Crowley befriended a French vintner, Georges de Latour, who had purchased acreage near St. Joseph's in order to plant grapes. De Latour and his wife, Fernande, were frequent visitors to the school and attended Sunday Mass at the chapel Father Crowley had established on the school grounds. Years later, the de Latours' winery,

Gardens at Round Pond Winery, where once St. Joseph's Agriculture Institute was farmed. *Courtesy of Lauren Coodley.*

Beaulieu Vineyard (BV), established in 1900, would buy grapes from the institute to make sacramental wine.

By 1915, St. Joseph's was in debt. Soon, the archdiocese began to subdivide and sell off the school lands. One of the buyers was Georges de Latour, who would use his acreage to plant vineyards. St. Joseph's finally closed its doors in 1928, the year that Father Crowley died. Despite national Prohibition in 1920, de Latour became one of the most successful vintners in California, thanks to his close ties to Crowley and the Catholic Church. Round Pond Winery is now at the site of the St. Joseph school. *Frankie's Journey: The Silk Road to Napa* is a book for children that tells this story.

FARM CENTERS FROM NAPA TO CALISTOGA

By 1923, the *San Francisco Chronicle* described Napa pears as reaching "a fine state of perfection." Napa's prize-winning pears were canned, dried and shipped green. Locally grown fruits and nuts (mainly prunes) were sold all over the country. Herman Baade, an agriculture teacher at Napa

The Tucker Farm Center was built in 1920 on the land of the Tucker family, who had settled south of Calistoga in the mid-1800s. *Courtesy of Napa County Historical Society.*

High School, helped to organize over a dozen centers where farmers met to share ideas. Napa County farm centers were in the following areas: Browns Valley, Los Carneros, Las Amigas, Coombsville, Salvador, Soscol and Oak Knoll, along with Rutherford Grange in Rutherford and the Tucker Farm Center in Calistoga. The *San Francisco Chronicle* reported, "These farm centers are also mediums for social interchange, 'getting acquainted' in a way that is pleasant and often produces life-long friendships."

These one-story buildings featured kitchens donated by farming families. Farm Advisors oversaw the transition from grain, oats and pasture to horticulture and, eventually, viticulture. 4-H was created during this period, out of concern for the isolation of rural children, and to teach citizenship and leadership. Ruby Flowers, a home economist, was an early leader of the Women's Auxiliary to the Farm Centers, where women learned to cover lampshades, stuff mattresses and can with pressure cookers. These centers eventually became the Farm Bureau.

JOHN BROWN'S VALLEY

Almost everyone who had a land grant in the Napa Valley lost most of it. Salvador Vallejo sold some of his land to settlers, but John Brown claimed that he purchased Brown's Valley for a horse and a buggy. Some people owned prune orchards in Browns Valley; others worked for them, picking fruit. In 1928, Olamae Wade Combellack recalled how, in 1928, her family rented a farmhouse where prune orchards stretched "as far as you could see." The house is still standing on Browns Valley Road across from what is now Karen Drive. In summer, kids' hands and knees were sticky with juice as they picked prunes, earning fifteen to twenty-five cents a box to buy school clothes.

Many Napa residents look back fondly to their lives in the fields and orchards in the 1920s. Peach and almond orchards owned by families such as the Hobsons, the Minahens and the Buhmans filled the area with pink and white blossoms in spring. Along with her mother, sisters and brothers, Olamae picked prunes. Eventually, Mary Wade became a harvest captain for some of the ranches. After harvest, the children attended Browns Valley School, then a one-room school with eight grades and twenty-six students

Olamae Wade's mother, Martine, a harvest captain for the prune farms in Browns Valley, with her prune harvest crew and employer Mr. McKenzie. *Courtesy of Olamae Combelleck.*

who were kept warm by a wood-burning stove. Olamae Wade Combellack fondly recalled skating down Browns Valley Road into downtown Napa without fear of being hit by cars.

SUNSWEET DEHYDRATOR, JACKSON STREET

In 1934, the Prune Association built its first automatic bulk-packing line. The most important development was the organization of the first cooperative dryer in Napa County. Mike Treleven describes it:

> *Back when prunes were the Napa Valley's star commodity, the Sunsweet Prune Packaging facility on Jackson Street was a bustling place. In the 1930s, Sunsweet was processing as much as 27,000 tons of prunes each harvest. In the plant's heyday, more than two hundred people worked there. The sweet scent of dehydrating prunes would hang over downtown Napa on autumn mornings. Prunes were billed as "God's pure air and fruit."*

The building has had many uses since Sunsweet shut down, including Rockzilla (a rock-climbing gym), TEM Machine Shop, Sunsweet Cabinetry, Copper Iron Designs and Jackson Street Wine Warehouse.

Old Sunsweet building next to railroad tracks, Napa, 2003. *Courtesy of Lauren Coodley.*

THE VON UHLIT FRUIT FARM, SOSCOL AND TRANCAS

Ruth Raeder and George von Uhlit had met at the Vichy Springs Pool in 1931 and married in 1933. With $2,000 in cash, they bought a forty-acre farm on Soscol Avenue just south of Trancas. Ruth gave birth to four children, all born at home. She rode horseback the day after her daughter was born. Ruth's heroine was Gertrude Ederle, who swam the English Channel in 1939. In tribute to that kind of determination, she and her husband built a swimming pool on their property, where Ruth von Uhlit taught hundreds of Napa children to swim. The von Uhlit farmers built a dehydrator and were drying prunes, ten tons a day. In addition to prunes, they grew apples, walnuts, pears, peaches, persimmons, almonds and apricots. Marilyn Warnock writes:

> *My first paying job other than baby-sitting was on their ranch grading pears. The Grade 1 pears went to market, and the others went to the cannery, and the culls went to baby food. Mr. von Uhlit was "Papa Georgie" to us, and Ruth was MOM. She used to ride a motorcycle to U.C. Berkeley, and got her teaching credential. I first met her at Napa High School, where she was substitute teaching. They had old barns and storage places on the ranch, and a wonderful antique square grand piano in the barn along with hundreds of other treasures, like buggies, and buckboards, and who knows what all.*

Readers of the *Napa Valley Register* in July 1995 learned that Ruth von Uhlit had died "surrounded by the tranquility of her much loved urban ranch with hummingbirds hovering outside her bedroom window." Kevin Courtney detailed the fight to preserve her home:

> *The city's last fruit farm survives in the memories of legions of locals who drove past the sentry eucalyptus trees on Soscol Avenue and up the long driveway to buy the freshest peaches, pears and apples in town. To loyal customers, the ranch and the woman who ran it were beloved vestiges of an earlier, more rural Napa. The city's Cultural Heritage Commission debated whether to let the von Uhlit ranch disappear without a physical trace. Historical consultants hired by the developer were unanimous that the ranch property did not meet the usual requirements for historical significance.*

Right: In 1923, Ruth Raeder moved to Napa, where her uncle was an orchardist for the Napa State Hospital. *Courtesy of Greta von Uhlit.*

Below: Von Uhlit orchard. For thirty-three years, Ruth taught citizenship classes and attended all citizenship swearing-in ceremonies. *Courtesy of Greta von Uhlit.*

John Wagenknecht describes von Uhlit with admiration as "the holdout against giving up farming because she had what she wanted." Yet her farm was razed, and apartments now crowd out to the street. Napa Nursing Center was once part of the von Uhlit ranch. In 2007, residents of the nursing center participated with enthusiasm in Diane Berg's class about local history. Larry Duncan remembered the swimming hole on Trancas, where fresh water was north of the bridge; south of it, the water was brackish and salty. He and his friends would cut across the von Uhlit property. He described Mrs. von Uhlit as "very nice, always giving children fruit." Later, Larry picked prunes for twenty-five cents a box to buy school clothes.

LUHMANN EGG FARMING, BIG RANCH ROAD

Beatrice and Henry Luhmann traveled by covered wagon in 1913 to Napa and pitched their tent downtown until they earned enough to buy the farm on Big Ranch Road. They lived their whole lives on that farm with crop failures and low prices for poultry. Beatrice wrote:

> *Planted a young orchard of prune trees, while we were waiting for fruit went into the chicken business. The babies survived, that meant more chickens.... To make ends meet we raised fryers, the wholesale price was so low we dress them, price 20 cents a pound...for the pan and delivered, that was my job, at the crack of dawn would get dressed from l to 3 in the morning and deliver in the afternoon.*

Henry Luhmann was an egg farmer who invented a particular kind of brooder. He was also a leader in the community of farmers that came together during World War II. He kept carefully typed minutes from a farm labor committee he chaired. At a meeting on June 17, 1943, Henry explained the progress made in securing housing facilities at the Silverado Farm Labor camp: "Andrew Fagiani suggested that part of the camp at Yountville be set aside for family groups....The chairman stated that Mr. DB Parker had offered to give Napa County a building located at the Stockton Japanese relocation center."

In July 1945, Henry Luhmann wrote to Dr. Theo Miller of the Napa State Hospital to say that the farm labor committee had been advised of the "splendid help the patients have been in past years in our harvest....We were also advised that you have again granted permission to certain patients

Left: Poster, "Some New Poultry Wrinkle." *Courtesy of Deb Jachens.*

Below: Henry and Beatrice Luhmann, around 1940. *Courtesy of Deb Jachens.*

to aid in our harvest again this year. Indications are that we will have a very heavy crop of prunes and tomatoes and every person who is able and willing to help with this harvest will find employment."

POW CAMP

Six months later, in June 1945, a new dilemma emerged for the committee. Clyde Casady, secretary of Napa Valley Farm Labor Corporation, wrote to Henry Luhmann, asking him to "lend every effort possible in helping us solve the problem of security measures at the Silverado Trail camp. This camp is to be used to house German prisoners-of-war....The prune and grape crops...look to have the greatest tonnage to be harvested in the history of the valley....With a definite shortage in Mexican nationals, the only other source of labor available is prisoners of war."

Ron Kyle remembers hearing about the German prisoner-of-war camp located on the Silverado Trail below Rector Dam: "The mother of some high school friends told me about this. She spoke German and would talk to them when they were out working on the roads. As a kid I remember seeing Quonset huts there and they always seemed a little out of place."

The Napa POW Camp was opened in 1945 at 7292 Silverado Trail. There is now a marker in its place that reads:

> *At the request of Great Britain, over 700 POW camps were built within the USA to help alleviate the overcrowding of British camps. On August 14, 1945, three months after Germany surrendered and the day before Japan surrendered, 250 prisoners were received at Camp Napa located on the Silverado Trail just north of Yountville. This was a branch facility of Camp Beale. Prisoners performed labor on surrounding farms and were paid $.80 per day. Local citizens often attended social activities in camp. At war's end, most prisoners repatriated to Germany. Many returned to the USA to renew acquaintances with their former "employers," start families, launch new careers, and become citizens.*

In April 1946, Henry Luhmann recorded "the amount of foreign labor in the county last year, reaching a peak of 345 Mexican nationals in July and a peak of 645 foreign laborers in August, including Prisoners of War and Jamaicans."

Beatrice Luhmann and her dog.
Courtesy of Deb Jachens.

After Henry's death, Beatrice still tended a garden and fruit trees. She used a special drying process for her figs, and she kept boxes of feathers from her chickens, separated carefully by colors. With those feathers, she decorated hats. In front of the farm was a thick plank painted with letters spelling "Luhmann"; her friend Marilyn Grover personally refreshed the sign. It is still there, the old name covered with the name of the new occupants, *JK Farm*.

THE BUILDING OF LAKE BERRYESSA AND THE DESTRUCTION OF MONTICELLO

Berryessa Valley was named after Jose Jesus and Sisto Berryessa, two brothers who obtained a Mexican land grant of about thirty-six thousand acres in 1843. They built a ninety-foot adobe and raised cattle and horses, but had to slowly sell off the land to pay gambling and other debts. In 1860, the last plot was auctioned off for $1,653.

Monticello was founded six years later. Three hundred people lived there. The annual springtime cattle roundup began in 1926; by the 1930s, thousands were traveling to the event. A massive barbecue pit would begin roasting locally grown cattle the night before the rodeo. Visitors could listen to John Phillip Sousa's band music performed live and watch bronco riding and wild-cow milking. Monticello Road carried freight wagons to and from the Berryessa Valley. Teams would line up at Milliken Creek off the Napa River on Trancas.

By 1943, the Berryessa Valley was producing the following output: nearly 3,000 tons of hay, about 1,000 tons of grapes, 700 tons of dried prunes, 1,000 tons of pears, 90 tons of plums, almost 4,000 tons of grain, almost 7,000 head of cattle, 2,000 head of sheep and 3,000 head of hogs. All of this production entailed about 45,000 man-hours.

Former park ranger at Lake Berryessa Paul Donovan recalls:

> *As early as 1906, proposals were being made to throw a dam across Putah Creek and create a vast reservoir in the Valley. It wasn't until the 1940s—1948—that the project made headway. After a 1951 bond issue to build a local dam upstream failed to pass, the Bureau of Reclamation with a $47 million appropriation launched its Monticello Dam. Berryessa was once a*

In the nineteenth century, produce wagons were hauled by mule teams with provisions for travelers. *Courtesy of Napa County Historical Society.*

Ad for Pears, 1920s. *Courtesy of Napa County Historical Society.*

> *valley so rich with grade I and II soils of fertile farmlands of the valley in which the town of Monticello was located, but it was not given up by the farmers without a fight. The valley stripped of trees, farm buildings, bridges, will soon be plain dusty steep slopes and a complete flat cleared floor that will soon be filled with the beautiful water as we see it today. All ranchers in the valley must face progress in motion and see Monticello and ranch homes gone forever.*

Peter Jensen writes: "Solano County, California Gov. Earl Warren, even officials in Washington, D.C., conspired to build Monticello Dam and force the removal of an agricultural community that had thrived since the mid-19th century….Napa County officials wanted to preserve Berryessa Valley for agriculture, while Solano interests wanted the valley's water for Solano's farms and cities."

The fight culminated in Congress in a series of hearings on a bill authorizing Monticello Dam in April 1948. Napa County was outgunned at the hearings. County Supervisor N.D. Clark called the project an "unnecessary and wanton destruction of deep, rich, fertile soil." The valley's crop production had a value of $1 million the year before, and the yields were uniformly high. Clark, the chairman of the Berryessa Valley Protective Association, stated: "The people of Berryessa Valley, and the town of Monticello, will be made homeless and forced to relocate to other districts at a tremendous loss to them….They will be scattered and separated, one friend from another, one relative from another, and let me say that some of these families have been established since pioneer days."

At the Vacaville Museum, a memorial to Monticello begins: "The residents of Berryessa Valley do not object to the development and the complete utilization of the water resources of the Putah Creek watershed in accordance with the recommendation of the State Engineers. But they feel that the fertile land and the valuable improvements in the Berryessa Valley should not be destroyed."

But the water source was declared to be necessary for national defense purposes and met the legal requirements for a federal reclamation project. Peter Jensen adds:

> *For residents of Berryessa Valley, the die was cast. The exodus of the valley's farm families would soon begin. "It changed my whole life," said Murray Clark, 79, a Berryessa old-timer. "It changed everybody's lives." The residents, ranchers and farmers left, the buildings were razed, the orchards cut down, the crops uprooted. Even the graves in the cemetery were exhumed and moved to higher ground. All that remained was the two-lane highway and the stone bridge—Napa County's longest—over Putah Creek. "We fought that thing as long as we could," Napa County Supervisor Brad Wagenknecht recently said of Monticello Dam. "We've been paying for it ever since."*

WEST PARK ORCHARDS, NAPA

The area west of downtown was all orchards in the 1940s and '50s. On West Park, where the Creekside Glen housing development now stands, Carolyn Knief's father grew three types of prunes, French, Imperial and Sugar, all of which were mid-sized. In the evenings, after he got home from work at Mare Island, and during his summer vacations, he, along with family and crew, stacked the boxes of prunes on a flatbed truck. They brought them to the barn area to be dipped in a lye solution and set out to dry on trays in the sun. Prunes that did not contain enough sugar would turn brown and shrivel. These brown prunes, called "chocolates," were picked from the trays and discarded. The good prunes were sold to the Sunsweet facilities in Napa. In addition to the prunes, the family also picked and sliced peaches. These were dried in a sulfa smoke and then sold to Sunsweet. Carolyn remembers:

> *I enjoyed spraying the prune trees to protect them from various diseases. Pop would fill the stray rig with water and the chemicals needed for the*

Ernest F. Knief Sr. and his daughters, Bethel and Carolyn, in front of their cherry orchard, 1942. *Courtesy of Carolyn Salazar.*

Carolyn Knief at bat, about 1953. Behind her are the windmill, the cornfield and the eastern hills. *Courtesy of Carolyn Salazar.*

spray. We would dress up in oversized rain slickers and hats, put some type of mask over our noses and mouths so that we would not breath in the chemicals, and climb up onto the top of the spray rig. Pop would drive his tractor, pulling the spray rig, up and down the rows of prune trees while we, holding nozzled hoses, would spray the trees. I also loved riding on the flatbed truck and helping gather the boxes of prunes, the evenings of dipping the prunes. I remember the nights when we would have a summer rain storm, and all the family would rush out to the fields to stack the trays of prunes so that they wouldn't get wet.

As Napa began to grow, it became more difficult to move the farm equipment across West Park Avenue to plow under the prune trees, so Knief sold the ten acres to the north of West Park Avenue in the late 1940s or early 1950s. He continued farming the other ten acres until about 1965, when he sold most of his land. Ernest Knief passed away in 1969, and Carolyn's mother, Lillian, in 1993. The family home, now on Bradford Street, still remains in the Knief family. Carolyn concluded: "Farming is not easy, and my dad's work at Mare Island helped to fully support his family, but I would not exchange the wonderful experiences of my childhood on our farm in Napa for anything. Working together as a family, enjoying the fresh fruits and vegetables grown, are things that many people cannot experience today."

DAVID WHEATLEY PRUNE FARM, YOUNTVILLE

Many of the orchards planted in the 1920s and '30s reached a point where they were in need of being replaced in the late 1960s and early '70s. Facing the prospect of tearing out the old orchards and replanting new crops, farmers chose the more economically profitable grapevines. By 1977, Louis Ezettie offered this poignant observation in his weekly newspaper column:

> *Once one of the great prune growing areas in the state, Napa County had seen the industry give way to an almost complete turnover to grape growing. Sunsweet disposed of the packing and shipping departments on Jackson Street, and reduced their workforce from 100 to 25 people. Napa Valley grown prunes, in my estimation, surpassed the quality of the fruit grown in other parts of the state. Every year we kids earned enough money picking prunes at the Frank Bush Ranch near Little Trancas to pay for school clothes and school books.*

This was the fate of most orchards, but a few determined farmers refused to switch to grapes. Stephanie Grohs describes one of them:

> *Ninety-year-old David Wheatley tasted alcohol once in his youth and didn't like it. He decided early on that he didn't want anything to do with growing grapes, making wine or "bootlegging." Driving on the private unpaved road to his farmhouse I was struck by the sharp contrast of the landscape. His land on the north side of the road is gently populated with prune and walnut trees in the open fields. Sitting with Mr. Wheatley in his back garden surrounded by trees and farm buildings, it is easy to visualize the valley when prune orchards reigned supreme. I could hear the pride in his voice as he talks about his life spent on this bountiful land. By his choice, the view on his side of the dirt road is unchanged.*

Today, 99 percent of agricultural land is dedicated to growing grapes. The few working farms exist to produce gourmet produce for the fanciest restaurants in town. People who live in Napa make their own gardens and often have fruit trees. The time when land was inexpensive and children could play in the country has been gone since about 1985. Many of the new arrivals to Napa will never see what John Wagenknecht remembers: looking over Napa each spring and seeing nothing but "blooms covered in

Above: Freight train by Sunsweet. *Courtesy of Lauren Coodley.*

Left: David Wheatley (*left*) and Mr. Eisley (*right*) of Sunsweet Growers, Wheatley orchard, September 1951. *Courtesy of David Wheatley.*

snow" on trees that would bear prunes, pears and peaches. Wagenknecht says "the conversion to monoculture was not healthy—but farmers were market driven and growing grapes always paid more money."

She drove a golf cart
across her property
like a goddess in her chariot:
spaniels at her heels, my
entranced child bouncing
alongside, barn to farmhouse.
She weighed the prunes she'd
dried, the peaches, pears, careless bounty
that once defined this valley,
and that she, defiant one, orchardess,
continued to grow—

and the old apples,
pippins, lay in their boxes,
her bounty, there and there,
speckling that open land
defying the condos and strip malls,
defying time, the fate of this valley
which is to forget its fruited past.

2

WHERE WE LIVED

Composed of a singular set of objects, each home occupies space and anchors lifetimes in the same way a tuft of grass catches and holds particles of soil.
—Joseph Amato, *Rethinking Home*

HOME OF ELIAS BARNETT, POPE VALLEY

Hearing of the vast land grants awarded by General Mariano Vallejo in Northern California, Julian Pope joined an expedition to the Napa Valley in 1841. Along with friends Cyrus Alexander, William Knight and William Gordon, he crossed the Carquinez Straits in a rowboat. They hired indigenous men to pilot them up the Napa River. After making base camp at Yount's home, in the area that would eventually be called Yountville, the four split up, each claiming a valley for his own. Pope petitioned General Vallejo and Manuel Casarin, the acting governor of California, for a parcel on the east side of Howell Mountain. The parcel, almost nine thousand acres, cost him twenty-five cents an acre. Pope named his grant "Rancho Locoallomi." Three schools—Central, Olive and Hardin—were located within William Pope's original 1841 land grant.

Pope's wife, Juliana, and their four children moved from Los Angeles and stayed at Yount's ranch while Julian built their first home on his new property. The Mexican government paid for the family's expenses, because it wanted the help of settlers like the Popes to subdue the indigenous population. In

Right: Jesse Barnett was the son of Elias Barnett, who married the first female settler of Pope Valley, Juliana Salazar Pope Barnett. *Courtesy of Napa County Historical Society.*

Below: Barnett house. *Courtesy of Napa County Historical Society.*

1842, at Yount's ranch, Juliana gave birth to her fifth child, Delavina. In 1843, the family moved wagons and livestock from Yount's ranch to their new adobe house, using ropes to ease the wagons down the steep trail. That same year, Julian was rushing to complete a wood house before winter and accidentally cut his leg when his ax slipped. According to one story, he was carried all the way to Sonoma for medical attention. Twelve days later, at the age of thirty-eight, he died.

Juliana was now thirty-three years old. The following spring, in 1844, she married her nearest neighbor, Elias Barnett, a Missouri pioneer who brought the first fruit tree seedlings from Missouri to Calistoga. Juliana

Pope Barnet took legal possession of Pope's land in 1845. In order to do so, she met the Mexican civil authorities with Elias, along with Florencio Salazar, Joseph Chiles and her surveyor, Juan Solis. Solis and George Yount, acting as surveyor for the mayor of Sonoma, measured the boundaries of the property. At each of the four corners of the property, Juliana pulled up stones and grass and threw them to the four winds, a ritual to declare her possession of the land.

In 1850, California was admitted as the thirty-first state in the union. In 1854, Juliana Pope Barnett sold half of the land and "100 head of cattle, 15 mares and 9 colts" to her eldest son for $8,000. She sold the other half of the land to her other five children for $5,000. At that point, she left Pope Valley, so perhaps she sold her land to finance her relocation. According to the Society of California Pioneers, her husband, Elias Barnett, died on February 8, 1880, in Pope Valley, where he had remained for all the years since Juliana moved away. Tucker Catlin explains: "The only structure still standing is the abandoned house of Elias Barnett, which sits on the east side of Pope Creek. It's actually pretty impressive and is famous for the stairway bannister which they brought from back east by wagon. Whether or not Juliana ever lived there, I don't know, but I'm pretty sure that Elias did."

The Pope Valley cemetery sits on Elias's land. A stone marks his burial site.

WILLIAM JACKS NURSERY, DOWNTOWN NAPA

William Jacks was a nurseryman, goldsmith, watchmaker and citizen of early Napa. He joined the flood of gold seekers to California in 1849. He hauled freight to the mines from Stockton before moving to San Francisco to operate his first jewelry and watch store. He was a partner from 1849 to 1850 in Jacks and Woodruff on Clay Street, the first jewelers, goldsmiths and silversmiths in San Francisco.

In 1847, Nathan Coombs and John Grigsby traded their carpentry skills to Nicholas Higuera, who paid for their services with land along the Napa River at the head of the tidewater. Coombs staked out a townsite from what is now Brown Street to the river and from Napa Creek to the foot of Main Street, a distance of about six hundred yards. Eventually, several land grants were combined to form the town of Napa: the land north of First Street, which had belonged to Salvador Vallejo; the land east of the river, which had belonged to Juarez and Rodriguez; and Higuera's grant west of the river that became downtown.

William Jacks, Napa town founder. *Courtesy of the Jacks family, public domain.*

In 1852, William Jacks bought land in Napa and built the first house on the Napa Abajo. An early map shows Levee Street (now Riverside Street) and Grant Street (now Brown Street). His house and nursery were located at the corner of Oak and Grant. The *Napa Daily Register* noted: "General Jacks has lately built a rockery in his garden on Grant Avenue which is a great curiosity in its way. Many colored stones are used in its construction, adding greatly to the effect, and on the top sits a goose through the bill of which flows a stream of water. Here and there are pots containing flowers, the whole forming a beautiful object."

Jacks traveled back and forth between Napa and San Francisco on the *Dolphin*, Napa's first steamboat. Early historian of Napa C.A. Menefee noted, "Col. W.S. Jacks still preserves the bell of the *Dolphin* as a relic," indicating the significance of this water journey in his life.

A public notice proclaimed the opening of a new watch and jewelry store on Main Street, where Messrs. Chase and Jacks "will be glad to wait upon customers." In 1855, Jacks was one of twelve organizers of the First Presbyterian Church on Third Street. When the first service was held, he presented a silver communion service set, still used today.

An 1856 article in the *Sacramento Daily Union* celebrated a gift of a box of fruit from the Jacks nursery:

> *The contribution included splendid specimens of the Bartlett Pear, Rambo, Newtown Pippin, Nectarines, Peaches of several varieties, Almonds, and Ground Cherries....Upon an arbor 400 feet in length, he has reared grapes of all varieties, and in addition to between 20 and 30 apple trees in full bearing...Apricots, Plums, Cherries, Currants, Gooseberries, Raspberries and Blackberries growing in the greatest profusion. The grounds are handsomely laid out, and kept at a proper degree of moisture by the simple flowing of the tide, it being unnecessary to irrigate at any season of the year. The nursery is conducted by the proprietor merely for recreation—not as a source of profit, the fruit being dispensed with a liberal hand to all visitors*

Above: Steamboat on the Napa River. *Postcard courtesy of Mr. M.*

Right: Silver Communion set made by William Jacks. *Courtesy of Lauren Coodley*.

without charge. The visitor can take a seat on a side porch of the General's mansion, and throw a line into the creek, haul in fish ad libitum.

William Jacks and his family lived the rest of their lives in the house on Brown and Oak Streets. The Jacks home was as elegant as the remaining Victorians on Brown Street. A magazine praised the enormous aloe and yucca plants that he grew (all irrigated by only river water). William Jacks died in 1890. The local paper mourned: "Another California pioneer has joined the army of the immortals; there is another vacant chair in one of Napa's quiet homes. Like one who folds the mantle of his couch about him and lies down to pleasant dreams he passed peacefully away in his easy chair. In a full age, like as a shock of corn cometh in his season, so he met the summons which all knew was not afar off."

The year of his death, a major rainstorm caused the river to flood. The Jacks house must have been lost in this flood; its site no longer exists as buildable land due to floods and landscape change. A marker at Oak and Brown Streets could mark the life of William Jacks, could even showcase the bell from the *Dolphin*. The bell's location is unknown at this time.

Near where the house once stood is Giovannoni's Market, an early Italian market now operated by the Magallanes family. Stately Victorians have been transformed into bed-and-breakfast inns, along with low-income apartments which now occupy that Riverside neighborhood.

SAM BRANNAN HOUSE AND STABLES, CALISTOGA

Sam Brannan had visited the spas of Europe and decided to set up his own California version in 1862. He named it Calistoga. The Brannan Cottage Inn stands at 109 Wappo. This cottage, which has a landmark distinction, was one of the first cottages built when Sam Brannan was establishing the original hot springs grounds in 1860. As popularity waned, some cottages became rented or purchased homes. Around 1980, the cottage was purchased and restored.

Sam Brannan's original resort included a large racetrack and stables for the horses. The stable itself was built in 1859 and is still in its original location. The stable sheltered horses belonging to Hearst, Hopkins & Lick Company, personal friends of Sam Brannan. Ephraim Light purchased the stables in 1915 and converted it to a winery, later sold to Napa Valley Cooperative Winery. Around 1960, it was used for bottling mineral water. The remainder of the racetrack property is now Calistoga High School, with its track.

Above: Brannan Cottage, now a hotel boutique bed-and-breakfast style, the only Brannan Cottage still in the original location. *Courtesy of Eden Umble.*

Left: Sam Brannan stables located on what is now Grant Street. *Courtesy of the Sharpsteen Museum.*

ROBERT LOUIS STEVENSON CABIN, MOUNT ST. HELENA

When Robert Louis Stevenson married Fanny Van de Grift Osbourne, his family cut off his trust fund. In Oakland to obtain Fanny's divorce from her first husband, the Stevensons could not afford any rent. Friends of Fanny mentioned Mount St. Helena at the upper end of the Napa Valley, because they knew the mountain contained several abandoned miners' cabins. Thus Calistoga became a destination for the Stevensons. On May 22, 1880, the couple arrived in the valley to enjoy what writer M.F.K. Fisher describes as a few "poignant and enchanted months in the Northern California valley named Napa by its vanished Indians." In his memoir of their visit, Stevenson offers a rare picture of the Napa Valley in the late nineteenth century:

> *Bucks, bears and rattlesnakes and former mining operations, are the staple of men's talk. Agriculture has only begun to mount above the valley and though in a few years from now the whole district may be smiling with farms, passing trains shaking the mountain to the heart, many windowed hotels lighting up the night like factories, and a prosperous city occupying the site of sleepy Calistoga; yet in the meantime, around the foot of that mountain the silence of nature reigns in a great measure unbroken.*

The newlyweds visited Jacob Schram, an early vintner, whom Robert Louis Stevenson immortalized in the book *The Silverado Squatters*. Stevenson commented that California wine was still in the experimental stages, but in the future would come the time when "the wine is bottled poetry." Leaving the Schrams, the Stevensons found an abandoned cabin near the deserted mine of Silverado. One advantage of this location was that it was above the valley fog that threatened Stevenson's health.

Determined to overcome the challenge of renovating an abandoned bunkhouse, the Stevensons were delivered by stagecoach to their new home on the mountain. Fanny mended the bunker while he wrote. While residing at Silverado, Stevenson would walk down to Lawley's Toll House to mingle with travelers bound for Lake County and occasionally even walk to Calistoga.

Robert Louis Stevenson. *Courtesy of Napa County Historical Society.*

A few months later, his parents relented, so the Stevensons returned to the British Isles. Stevenson immortalized the Napa Valley with the publication of *The Silverado Squatters* in 1883 and also recalled Mount St. Helena in *Treasure Island*, perhaps his most famous work. Published in 1883, the novel contains a description of the island and its peaks. Stevenson wrote that Treasure Island contained "many tall trees, of the pine family, outtoping the others—some singly, some in clumps....The hills ran up clear above the vegetation in spires of naked rock. All were strangely shaped, and the Spyglass, which was by three or four hundred feet the tallest on the island, was...suddenly cut off at the top like a pedestal to put a statue on."

This describes Mount St. Helena in almost every respect. Today, Mount St. Helena is called Robert Louis Stevenson Memorial State Park. Although nothing remains of Stevenson's cabin, the site is identified on the trail to the summit.

Stevenson next wrote *A Child's Garden of Verses*, published in 1885. Within this beautiful collection are suggestions of the influence of the Napa Valley. Cherry trees grew plentifully in this "foreign land." Stevenson writes:

> *I saw the dimpling river pass*
> *And be the sky's blue looking-glass;*
> *The dusty roads go up and down*
> *With people tramping into town.*
> *If I could find a higher tree*
> *Farther and farther I should see*
> *To where the grown-up river slips*
> *Into the sea among the ships.*

CHINESE NEIGHBORHOODS, NAPA AND ST. HELENA

In 1868, the Napa Valley Railroad construction crews reached St. Helena. They needed large amounts of gravel from a quarry to lay down the base for the tracks. Although a few Chinese were previously living in Napa, the need for a labor force to move gravel brought the first large group of Chinese immigrants to the upper Napa Valley. They were housed where they worked, next to the gravel pit, now owned by Harold Smith & Sons.

The Chinese neighborhood was located on what is now West Charter Oak Avenue, set back from Main Street and parallel with it. Chinese were not allowed to own property; their landlord was John Gillam, who provided hastily thrown-up shacks made of scrap lumber. Buildings were constructed of old shingles, broken packing boxes and flattened kerosene cans. By 1870, there was a "China store" and a Cantonese restaurant. By 1884, there were boardinghouses, a hotel, more stores, the employment office and a Taoist temple.

The Taoist temple, completed in 1891, was located at the western end of the neighborhood. A grand dedication was held, with entertainment

In the late 1800s, Chinese laborers arrived by the hundreds to pick blackberries every July; more came for the hop harvest in August. *Courtesy of Napa County Historical Society.*

by a Chinese band from Napa. During the three days, ten roast pigs were consumed by the over one hundred attendees. The interior consisted of a large table with a bronze pedestal topped by a gold-mounted dragon, surrounded by four bronzed vases and several incense burners. On both sides of the room were two long boards artistically painted and engraved with the names of the Napa and Calistoga members. The building cost $5,000, all donated.

Local residents often attended the elaborate funerals. When Lee Hau, a prominent St. Helena resident, was killed by a falling tree at Niebaum's farm in 1894, his funeral was attended by many locals. The body was conveyed to the cemetery with a procession consisting of a wagon filled with foods for the afterlife, a hearse accompanied by six Chinese men and fifty men wearing bands of red and white. There were about ten vehicles and another band at the end. A Chinese section at the cemetery contained a large number of plots near the creek. It was important to every Chinese man to be buried with his ancestors. The bodies of those who could afford it were exhumed later

Above: Chinese children living in Napa, early twentieth century. *Courtesy of Napa County Historical Society*.

Right: Shuck Chan donated the Joss House altar to the Chinese Historical Society in San Francisco. *Courtesy of Napa County Historical Society*.

and sent home. A series of fires damaged Chinatown and finally destroyed it completely by 1911.

In Napa, the Chinese community consisted of rows of wood buildings between the Napa Creek and the Napa River. The two-story Joss House, or Taoist temple, was both a spiritual and a social center. Chan Wa Jack, who arrived in the 1870s, helped build the Joss House, where sandalwood candles burned and peanut oil fueled glass lanterns. Its altar arrived in Napa on a sailing ship, along with a wood scroll reading, "Your blessings are spread out to embrace us all." The two hundred Chinese men who worked at the Sawyer Tannery, along with those who built stone fences along Silverado Trail, created hand-carved pieces to decorate the altar.

The Chinese also established a steam laundry, a barbershop and a grocery store. A red-uniformed Chinese band performed at funerals and New Year's festivals. There is a separate graveyard for the Chinese at Tulocay Cemetery. The opium pipe repairman had his own shop: the pipes were made of hollow bamboo with ivory mouthpieces. In 1898, Wa Jack went to Weaverville, where he married a bride from China; they returned to town with their three-year-old son, Shuck Chan. Shuck Chan later went to China for an arranged marriage, came back to Napa in 1932 and opened a business on First Street called the Lai Hing Company, which offered Chinese nuts, candies and other delicacies.

In the winter of 1930, Mayor Charles Trower launched a campaign to clean up the Napa River. Frequent mysterious fires between 1915 and 1930 had already forced many Chinese residents out. City officials removed their wood dwellings and renamed the area China Point Park. For decades, it was a beautiful location.

Timothy Murphy recalls: "There were cool shops and funky businesses all over downtown. It was a great time to grow up here! I purchased a beautiful small brass opium pipe in the late sixties at an antique shop in downtown Napa. It had engraving on its side. It also had a little compartment beside the pipe with a brass lid."

By 2000, under the Flood Control Plan, the First Street Bridge and China Point Park were scheduled to be demolished. Al Edminster, a volunteer at the Napa Firefighters Museum, led a campaign in 2003 to save them. Lorraine Dong, of the Chinese Historical Society of California, wrote to the Napa City Council: "Napa's China Town has special significance for the Society. For many, China Point might appear as just another Chinatown, but it is valuable in providing us with another affirmation of an early Chinese settlement in America's West." Ultimately, Edminster was victorious in

Buildings in Chinese neighborhoods were constructed of old shingles, broken packing boxes and flattened kerosene cans. *Courtesy of Napa County Historical Society.*

Sam Kee Laundry is now a wine bar. *Courtesy of Napa County Historical Society.*

preserving the bridge, which was relocated, but the trees in China Point Park were cut down to make way for new bridge construction in 2008. By 2020, even the multiplex that had replaced Napa's old movie palaces had been swept away; what remains are expensive, brand-name stores aimed at tourists and one last department store, once Mervyns, now Kohl's. Plans were just approved to transform Kohl's into a hotel complex.

ITALIAN NEIGHBORHOOD, NAPA

Cousins Nelly Lagorio and Uriglia Magini grew up in a neighborhood that had been Juarez's Tulocay Grant and was now Napa's "Little Italy." Little Italy consisted of several blocks from a small portion of Third and Fourth Streets to Silverado Trail and up the hill, including lower Alta Heights and parts of First Street north to Spring Street.

Italian houses had two kitchens, one in the basement and one on the first floor, in case of flooding. Nelly married Dave Cavagnaro, and they eventually ran his father's business, the Brooklyn Hotel, which came to be known as "Dave's Place." Lou Guisto recalled:

> *I was born in the Brooklyn Hotel, next to the railroad tracks. My mom ran the hotel; my dad worked for the railroad and then he raised potatoes off Coombsville Road. They were boarding hotels for Italian people. Most*

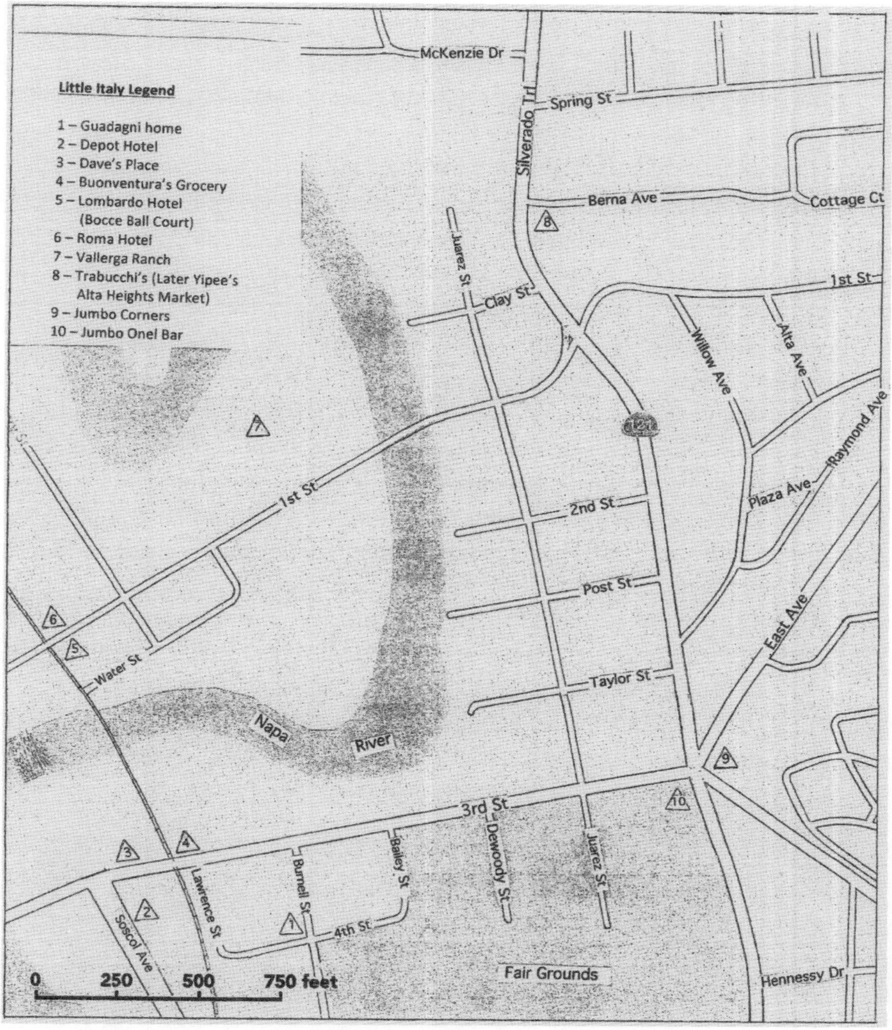

Map of Little Italy. *Courtesy of Ray Guadagni.*

of the men didn't marry. They would get together and sing and play bocce ball. Our brother, Dave, was a grand man. He used to help the Italians a lot. Every room had boot jacks. They wore leather boots in those days and you needed the jack to get them off.

The families on Third and Fourth Streets in Ray Guadagni's immediate neighborhood were the Guistos, Marchinis, Buonventuras, Grattones, Martinis, Squicciarinis and Pittores. Guadagni recalls:

> *It seemed to me that everyone was Italian in Napa....No matter how small one's backyard was, everyone had an Italian garden of vegetables and herbs, including plenty of basil, garlic and rosemary. If space allowed, there were fruit trees as well. My best friend Paul Vallerga's family ranch on First Street produced enough food to feed their large family; additionally, they could fish in the Napa River, located behind their ranch. They even had chickens and cows. What they couldn't grow or raise on their ranch, they obtained by bartering.*

Ray began playing the accordion when he was five: "My lessons were given in the basement of Mrs. Cameron's house by Willie Ferranato, also Italian. I must admit I was cute as a bug's ear. I was usually dressed in old clothes from the Martini or Guisto trunk."

As recently as 1973, Napa's Italian heritage was remembered and celebrated. Napa College marked "Italian Culture Week" on March 27 of that year with a program that included Terry Lamb's direction of drama students reading aloud. Andrew Rogerio and Hank Zwetsloot played Italian music on guitar and mandolin, June Schaal's class demonstrated Italian folk dances, Leo deVita presented slides on Italy and Gregory Rodeno was

Ray Guadagni with accordion. *Courtesy of Ray Guadagni.*

the master of ceremonies. On March 28, Nancy Burris sang operatic arias, Hanna Cassell directed Italian students from Napa High in a play and Luigi Zanardi played the accordion. Mary Doud, owner of Family Drug, was the mistress of ceremonies. By Friday, March 30, an Italian dinner was offered for two dollars, Betty Hagedorn sang operatic arias, and Frank Altamura exhibited art in the lobby of the Little Theatre. Sponsors of the event included Italian businesses ranging from Primo Collo's Shell Service, Roy Rota's Riverside Service Station, Rossi's Grocery, Ruffino's Restaurant, Al Zanardi's Bel Aire and Pometta's Food and Poultry from Oakville. None of these businesses remain open today.

KINCAID HOUSE, BROWNS VALLEY

In 1926, Ernest Kincaid delivered mail in the Italian part of town. Muriel Dunn taught Latin and Spanish at Napa High School. She left that job to marry Ernest in 1929. Together, they designed and built a house at what became 2724 Browns Valley Road. Later, the right-of-way was named Easum Drive, after Muriel's mother's maiden name. Like everywhere in Napa, there were orchards of prune, walnut, peach and pear. A creek overflowed in winter and dried up in summer. Soon, there were steps down to the creek bank and grapevines, some strong enough to use as swings over the water. Ernest and Muriel planted a garden that produced potatoes, green beans, watermelons, cantaloupes and artichokes. The family grafted eleven varieties onto three apple trees. To the north, along the creek, the family grew wheat and corn. "Sometimes," their son Nilan remembers, "Sunday breakfast would include pancakes or waffles made from freshly ground wheat or corn. What a treat! Very filling!"

Ernest Kincaid with sons Nilan and Gary, 1936. *Courtesy of Nilan Kincaid.*

By 1935, Ernest Kincaid was promoted to assistant postmaster. Nilan Kincaid explained that before Napa had dial telephone service, Pacific Telephone employed operators "who, when the light for a particular line number flashed, would say 'Number Please.'" Residents outside city limits (to the west, these limits were just past Ornduff Street, now known as California Avenue) had farmer line service. Kincaid provides the details: "Each phone circuit required two separate wires, suspended from telephone poles. Service to Dunn Lee Manor was 21F3, i.e., 3 rings....Each subscriber would get the operator by turning a hand crank and every subscriber powered his own phone with dry cell batteries, 3 inches in diameter and 6 inches tall."

Nilan remembers that the family raised chickens during the war:

> *It fell to the boys in the family to feed and water the chickens, clean the droppings, and collect and clean the eggs. Their father would estimate the size of the eggs and pay his sons the wholesale egg prices published in the Napa Register. Any eggs beyond family needs would sometimes be sold to the neighborhood store* [now the 7-11 on Browns Valley Road]. *The family also maintained rabbit hutches that could accommodate 4 to maybe 6 of the critters....Not bad eating.*

In 1943, Ernest Kincaid hired the first female mail carrier on the West Coast, Leila Hansen. For a while, the Kincaids boarded her in their spare room until she was able to rent an apartment on 1218 Elm Street, right near Kiwanis Park. Nilan, then thirteen, biked over to visit Mrs. Hansen and her daughter Carol. He found Carol up in an oak tree with a neighbor named Barbara Rosebrook. He and Barbara dated all through high school.

Near the end of World War II, there were ten families on the Browns Valley 21F line. Nilan writes, "It is amazing that this writer was able to use 21F3 to have extended phone conversations with the young lady who was to be his bride for 54 years." Following the end of the war, copper was again available for telephone service until, one by one, Pacific Telephone took over the rural telephone companies. Pacific Telephone removed the wire from the poles, and those who wanted part of it, got it. The Kincaid family took two large rolls, each about five feet in diameter and at least five hundred feet long: "Useful for low band amateur radio antennas," comments Nilan Kincaid.

By 1954, Ernest Kincaid had become postmaster, a position he held until his retirement in 1960. Nilan Kincaid recalls the situation throughout the 1960s:

> *When it would have been prudent for the owners to live their remaining years elsewhere, the property was listed for sale. Yet, the lady of the house*

Left: Muriel and Ernest Kincaid in 1968. *Right*: Dunn Lee Manor. *Courtesy of Nilan Kincaid.*

> *did not want to leave her beloved Dunn Lee Manor. If a prospective buyer had children, she would tell them how dangerous the creek was for children. Even after the adjoining property to the west was sold, she asked those buyers to rescind the transaction; this they refused to do.*

After the deaths of Muriel Kincaid and her husband, by 1976, Dunn Lee Manor sold for about $77,000. Decades later, Nilan Kincaid visits Napa regularly. He always comes to Easum Drive, where the house is now a bed-and-breakfast called Candlelight Inn.

DOWNTOWN NAPA

Olamae Wade was three years old when a flood washed her family's house down a river in Texas. They journeyed to Napa in 1924, pitching a tent at Gardner's Auto Camp along Napa Creek downtown. Just south of the auto camp was South Franklin Street, a neighborhood of tanners, paper hangers, stevedores and rivermen. Edna and Rita Guisti grew up there, on a street that is now Riverside Drive, and went barefoot all summer, wearing cotton dresses with bloomers underneath. They climbed the big oak tree on Oak Street and swung out over the river on its rope swing.

Jane Smith was born in 1922 and grew up at 1915 Second Street, a home that she visited in 2003 to find "ghosts still sitting in the chairs." She writes, "I learned to love the neighborhoods of old Napa during my long career

Top: Olamae Wade (*right*) with her mother, Mary Etta Wade, and siblings. *Courtesy of Olamae Combellack.*

Bottom: Browns Valley orchards. *Courtesy of Robert Northrup.*

as a piano student. On lesson days, I found the shadiest streets and learned where to swipe loquats, plums, and snapdragons. I knew who would be out on their front porches, from Mayor Oliver Hoffman to the ladies who sat outside all summer."

Jane recalls that there was only one policeman, and "he went home at night." In her recollection of Depression summers in downtown Napa, she says: "There weren't that many cars. Or people. The neighborhoods were clustered close around the town." She remembers quiet summer days when "you watched for the tar to soften up in the street and come up bubbles. Then chewed it. Mr. Schambacher delivered French bread twice a week. He drove up front, round, rosy, plump, shyly smiling. First Street on the west stopped where the orchards began. Browns Valley Road was all country, flanked by prune trees, and only a few farmhouses."

SHIPYARD ACRES, SOUTH NAPA

Next to the State Hospital was Shipyard Acres, built during the war for military families and shipyard workers. Mildred Collins recalls,

> *The prolific farm and orchards of the Napa State Hospital were adjacent to the Acres. To the south—what is now Napa's industrial park—lay a*

Shipyard Acres. *Courtesy of Napa County Historical Society.*

wonderful marshland filled with flocks of singing blackbirds, both solid black and red-winged. Frogs took over the chorus on cool, breezy nights; nights when the stars and moon seemed close enough to reach up and touch. The tract was pretty much a self-contained village and a godsend for World War II vets and families who had endured transient lives along with less than desirable housing all during the war. The kitchen-dining areas had large pantries equipped with a stationary rinsing tub and space for a washing machine. We'd been lucky enough to find a used square-tubbed Maytag with an excellent ringer...a blessing compared to washboards. Detergent and instant starch had been unheard of yet. There was a grocery store that stocked the basics. And over on the west side of town, Stewart's Dairy sold glass gallon containers of unpasteurized milk with a thick topping of pure sweet cream. The store had lots of penny candies and a very tolerant staff. Without encumbering fences, kids were free to roam.

GREEN MEADOWS, IMOLA AVENUE

Just north of Shipyard Acres were meadows that had once been the Spreckels Horse Breeding Farm. Spreckels Ranch, founded in 1898, originally stretched from Foster Road to the river and included what is now the River Park Shopping Center. In 1942, Andrew "Bar" and Alfreda "Mimi" Sheveland bought the four-hundred-acre stock farm for $100,000. In 1948, the Valley Horseman's Association purchased almost thirty-two acres and the milking barn from Andrew Sheveland for $19,100.

Part of the land was sold in 1948 for a housing tract that was called Green Meadows. It was by the river, green and meadow-like. Scott Sedgley has memories of growing up in Green Meadows:

My folks' first home in Napa was 2364 Bohen Street. We moved there in 1956. Our playground was the river and pasture lands of Sheveland and Stewart's. Every day two buses of men dressed in grey shirts and pants left and returned from Mare Island....There was a loose board in the fence that divided Sheveland Ranch from Green Meadows. I used to crawl through the space created by the loose board and play with Erica Valentine at Sheveland Ranch. We watched the KVON drive-in screen from our backyard.

Tanya Trolinder Berry adds: "I grew up on Barry Street in the seventies, best time ever. All our neighborhood friends are family; we were known as

Adolph Spreckels raised show horses, including the famous Seabiscuit, at his estate just south of downtown Napa (now River Park). *Courtesy of Mr. M.*

the Green Meadows gang. We knew when our dad whistled, you could hear it three streets away, it was time to get home."

In 2005, Sheveland Ranch was developed into luxury housing.

EAST NAPA, MADDELENA AND GRANT FARMS

Land was inexpensive in the valley until the 1990s. Even people of modest means could own a home in the country and raise their children there. The plain farmhouses, the rusting equipment, the quiet meadows are too often destroyed. Beautiful downtown Victorians are not the only homes Napans once inhabited, yet they often define Napa's history.

Linda McElroy writes a description of her family's land, at 1111 Terrace Drive:

> *My grandparents John and Theresa Maddalena purchased a three-acre farm for $8,000, in 1943...a two bedroom house, two car garage, four small rentals, one and a half acre pasture for the milk cow, chicken house, rabbit house, feed and shop rooms. Built in 1935 mostly of redwood, the buildings are in decay. My family is now pushing to bulldoze and sell to a*

Above: Farm at Terrace Drive, bunkhouse. *Courtesy of Carolyn Younger.*

Left: Farm at Terrace Drive, workshop. *Courtesy of Carolyn Younger.*

developer. . . . I am on a familial archaeological dig, becoming more involved each day. . . . I have great rabbit coop doors, farm implements, and I have not explored the garage loft yet. Most recent treasures: my grandfather's copper still, which he used for making grappa, a stationary box with letters from Italy written 1910–1922.

Although the Maddalena farm was sold in 2009, before Linda McElroy passed the keys to the new owner, she generously made the farm available to students working on the Napa Grid Project.

Mary Healey traveled by ferry every day from Vallejo to her office job on Mare Island. She and the ferry owner's son, Nay Raahauge, fell in love and got married. After their two daughters were born, they bought a farm at 1242 Hagen Road in 1937, where they opened the Hagen Road Dairy. The house was originally built in the 1820s, part of the Tulocay land grant.

They pulled out some of the prune trees and put in a barn for the cows. Their daughter Carol named the cows Doris and Betty and milked them by hand. Her family churned butter and sold milk in glass bottles to customers at their Dairy Drive-in.

Carol's mother died when she was fourteen. She maintained a lifelong friendship with Hilde Dusen and Connie MacLean. When they were Napa High students, they took the Greyhound bus to San Francisco to shop for school clothes, buying the newest styles of bathing suits to display at Vichy Springs Resort.

When Carol left for college, her father moved out of the home, leaving behind her mother's precious rose garden. In the sixties, she and her husband, Bob Grant, bought a portion of the family land and moved back

Carol Raahauge (*right*) in 1951 with best friends Hilde Dusen and Connie MacLean (*left*), taken at the county fair. Carol grew up on Hagen Road Dairy. *Courtesy of Connie MacLean Venturi.*

into her old house originally built in the 1820s. She went looking for her mother's rose garden. Hidden there under the brambles, she discovered the remaining three rose bushes. Inspired by her mother's memory, she restored the roses. Eventually, she had the largest garden in the valley with a thousand rose bushes. She named it the Secret Garden and sold flowers at a shed on her land until her own passing in 2000.

The house remains in private ownership, no longer with the Grant family.

BOURN MANSION, ST. HELENA

Greta Ericson moved to St. Helena in 1965: "We happened to be fortunate enough to be able to lease the old Bourn mansion on Sulphur Springs Road. A big red house, it was wonderful, on the corner of Crane and Sulphur Springs. We lived there sixteen years always thinking we would buy it, but the heirs to the Bourn family really decided to keep it and we then moved into town."

The property was part of the Bourn family estate, a country residence for one of San Francisco's most successful families during the time of California's gold rush. When the Bourns purchased the St. Helena property in 1872, the estate—which the family called Madroño—included over one hundred acres of vineyards, orchards and grazing pastures, two cottages and a home. Sarah Esther Bourn ran the estate after her husband's death and joined the efforts in silkworm cultivation that were also part of St. Joseph's Institute. The Bourns replaced the original house with a larger home, complete with Victorian towers and decorative stonework, which burned down in 1888. A second home was completed in 1903–4 and still stands on the property today.

Bourne House. *Courtesy of Marciano Estate.*

Marciano Estate, 2233 Sulphur Spring Avenue. *Courtesy of Marciano Estate.*

The Bourns' son William Bourn II and his partner, E. Everett Wise, built Greystone Cellars in 1888–89, today the home of the Culinary Institute of America's West Coast campus. Though the onset of phylloxera caused the sale of Greystone in 1894, the Bourn family continued to maintain their residence at Madroño, selling grapes to wineries throughout the valley.

Madroño remained in the Bourn family through successive generations, and though parcels of the property were split off and handed down to various descendants, the home and surrounding sixty acres remained in family hands until the late 1950s, when it was sold to the Christian Brothers, which had also purchased Greystone Cellars.

In 1972, Greta Ericson joined the chamber of commerce and, in 1973, became its president. In 1974, she ran for a seat on the city council. She recalled:

> *In those days, if you got the most votes, you were automatically the mayor, and I did get the most votes....I had the dress shop in town and knew every woman that came in to be fitted for one thing or another. It was a very definite edge....It gave me great satisfaction to pull all of the parking meters out of town and change the façade of St. Helena. I'm responsible for saving the Tunnel of Trees. They were supposed to be marked to be cut down, and I had all the children in the town write letters....We had almost 3,000 letters and stopped it right there...and we still got the trees so that's wonderful.*

In 1994, the Bourn family estate was purchased by the Bradley family, who sold the property to Maurice Marciano in 2006. He writes: "I'll never forget the first time I visited the property that would become Marciano Estate. It was a cool, clear day in January, and as I walked up the hillside behind the home and barn I came upon a stand of Douglas fir trees perched above the 20-acre vineyard. I stopped in my tracks. All of a sudden I had a feeling. This was it, this is where I belong."

FRANCIS HOUSE, CALISTOGA

James Francis, a merchant who operated the mercantile on the corner of Lincoln and Washington, owned several ranches, including one producing silver ore north of town. He commissioned a house at 1403 Myrtle Street. Sparing no expense, he contracted with architect John Sexton to build a Second Empire home out of stone quarried nearby, standing twenty-six feet high and finished inside with curled redwood and white paint. His brother G.M. Francis owned the *Napa Register*. The home was sold after the death of James Francis in 1891 to M.E. Billings. In 1906, Billings described the mansion as equipped with the latest material luxuries, including electricity, hot and cold running water and indoor bathrooms upstairs and downstairs.

In 1918, after Billings died, the house was converted into the Calistoga Hospital, open until 1964. After that, it became a site for illicit courtship and drug use and was almost demolished despite its placement in the National Register of Historic Places. The house was purchased in 2015 by Dina and Richard Dwyer, who renovated it into a beautiful bed-and-breakfast named the Francis House.

Francis House, 1886. *Courtesy of Dina and Richard Dwyer.*

Francis House Bed and Breakfast. *Courtesy of Dina and Richard Dwyer.*

Leonore Wilson grew up and lived on a working cattle ranch acquired by her grandmother in 1919 in Capell Valley. She describes her home, tragically lost in the August 2020 wildfire:

We walked the acreage of my motherland,
the attendant trails, parched, dusty
summer vetch spilling over the exhausted
gullies bursting with stone
and weed, the occasional godhead
of a golden poppy. On paths scarred with hoof,
domestic and wild, we lay down,
the chaff threshing our hands
as the body curved and fastened
and the sweet must of scat,
the little blades of obsidian
hoisted us upwards, the ridges
and hollows of prints mottling
our bellies, our backs, meaning the land
was stamping us with passage....

3
WHERE WE WORKED

They never—we never—thought any of it would change.
The river would never be diked and redirected to avoid
a mythical flood which will never happen again.
The workers at Basalt and Mare Island and Napa State Hospital
will have those jobs forever: we'll always need steel
and ships, and asylums, won't we?
—Lauren Coodley, "Shrimp Boat"

SODA FACTORY, SODA CANYON ROAD

Silverado Trail had long been used by indigenous peoples to walk up and down the valley. After the discovery of gold, twenty-seven springs of mineral-rich cold water about seven miles north of Napa City were claimed by Amos Buckman in 1855. By then, the indigenous population of Napa had been largely decimated by epidemics or displacement to Sonoma or Lake Counties. Buckman saw the commercial potential of the location. Doctors and resort owners, as well as the public, attributed many cures and health benefits to the use of therapeutic mineral waters.

By July 1856, the first resort hotel had opened at the springs, owned by San Francisco lawyer Eugene Sullivan and run by W. Allen. In 1860, the earliest known ad promoting the water at the spa appeared in the *Napa Reporter*.

On April 6, 1872, the *Reporter* announced that Colonel J.P. Jackson had bought the property for $120,000. By 1874, he had built a health and pleasure resort. Visitors to the hotel could view a wide stretch of the valley. Nearly all the buildings were constructed from stone quarried in the mountains nearby.

Napa Soda Springs contained mineral water of health-giving properties. On July 3, 1875, the *Napa County Reporter* ran a story about the technology involved in bottling gaseous water. A new bottling building had been constructed, and the springs were putting out more than three hundred dozen bottles a day. Local resident Charles Allen had discovered how to carbonate and bottle water to sell it commercially.

On January 15, 1886, the *Register* reported that the springs would be open year-round, a great stimulant to the local economy—"what was good for Napa Soda Springs was good for Napa." On May 21, 1892, the *Register* reported that on the previous Friday, the springs had shipped fifteen hundred dozen bottles, the most ever in one day. Seven wagons were required to haul the water down to the depot.

The bottling plant with all the latest equipment was situated in the main resort area. The water was bottled and capped on the premises. It was widely advertised for both alcoholic drinks and lemonade. On February 19, 1895, the *Napa Register* reported the wonders occurring at the springs, suggesting that the tallest century plant ever known in California was blooming, reaching almost forty feet in height, and that the bottling plant was shipping two million bottles annually.

Napa Soda Springs. *Courtesy of Kerry Creech.*

On July 18, 1897, the *Napa Daily Journal* noted that San Francisco saloons had recently run out of Napa Soda. The emergency was met by an all-night shift at the bottling plant and a delay of the steamer *Napa City* so the needed bottles could be stowed aboard.

On September 26, 1900, Colonel Jackson suddenly died, leaving the property to his wife. That century, the Soda Springs Resort began a slow decline. The First World War and Prohibition led to the closing of its doors to guests. Napa Soda—or "Jackson's Napa Soda"—continued to be sold through the Second World War, despite a devastating wilderness fire in the 1940s (it spared the bottling plant). In the fifties, Napa Soda Lemonade was served at the Gilt Edge in Napa, where Cathy Mathews remembers ordering it. The resort has never been restored. The plant itself was burned in an arson fire in the early 1960s. A visitor to the site will find nothing to indicate its former splendor. Fenced off from Soda Canyon Road, all that remains is the stone archway that once greeted visitors from around the Bay Area and the nation.

NAPA STATE HOSPITAL, HIGHWAY 29 AND IMOLA

California chose Napa in the 1870s as the place to build the 192-acre asylum, because the land was so inexpensive. The state bought 204 acres of the original Tulocay Mexican land grant from Don Cayetano Juarez for $15,000. The area included a wharf, a siding at the railroad tracks, a duck ranch and all of what is now Skyline Park. Promoters exploited the similarities between California and Italy and named the spot for the Italian city Imola, and it became an adjacent section of the town of Napa. This placed the hospital just south of town and close to the river. Patients worked on the farming and maintenance operations, sewed clothing, crocheted, knitted, embroidered, wove baskets and colonial mats and made items of brass, copper and clay, which the hospital either used or sold.

Eventually, hospital acreage totaled two thousand, from the Napa River to the eastern skyline. The early asylum, which locals called "The Farm," was nearly self-sustaining, with live-in staff, vegetable fields, orchards, cattle, a bakery and a wharf on the Napa River to receive supplies. In addition, patients, as late as the 1920s, still made the trip up the river in wicker cages secured to the boat deck. Because the founders believed that farming was therapeutic, patients raised their own vegetables, meat and dairy products

The Napa Asylum was renamed the Napa State Hospital in 1922. *Courtesy of Napa County Historical Society.*

and operated an award-winning pigsty. The patients also tended the orchards on the hospital grounds.

Built between 1875 and 1930 were nineteen staff and patient residences, eight maintenance and farm structures and six dams, along with the paving of several roads and the construction of a bus shelter—all with patient labor and bricks made on-site. Cog rails were installed in the basement to transport laundry and food to each of the buildings, maintenance shops, farm structures, officers' homes, employees' residences and garages. Additional property was purchased. At its peak, the facility occupied over two thousand acres.

Napans in the 1920s were fascinated by the asylum, which the State of California renamed Napa State Hospital in 1922. Jane Smith remembers the ball games attended by Napa townspeople, who watched the inmates play inside a fenced field. She remembers her neighbor, Abbey Halteman, who worked as a nurse there:

> *She drove a sporty Ford and sat up high in the driver's seat, erect as a queen in her carriage. She wore her silver hair coiled in a bun on top of her head held by tortoise shell hairpins and her nurse's cap on top of her bun....I admired her beautiful working clothes, the long-sleeved black and white striped uniform covered by a starched white apron, white shoes and the cap. She worked every day at the hospital, a turreted mysterious place where the corridors of the main building were hushed, where the floors shined with wax and the waiting room was graced with green potted palms...the very picture of a place of rest and healing, but a madhouse nonetheless....People like Abbey Halteman were the guardian angels of the mad.*

After World War II, all of the women working in blue-collar jobs at Mare Island were laid off. When Margaret Almstrom lost her job, she got hired at the Napa State Hospital to work the night shift. Only one nurse worked on her ward: "Whoever was on the ward had to be ready for anything to happen; no training was provided to handle mental patients. We had to sew

Napa State Hospital, 1930s. The history of the hospital is beautifully described in *Confessions of Madame Psyche* by Dorothy Bryant. *Courtesy of Cathy Mathews.*

Margaret Almstrom began working at the state hospital in the 1950s. *Courtesy of Margaret Almstrom.*

our own uniforms; they couldn't be purchased anywhere; I wore a white uniform fashioned into a one-piece dress and a nurse's hat."

For half a century, the main employer in Napa was the Napa State Hospital. Almost everyone knew someone who was a psych tech or a nurse there. To Napans, it was still known as Imola—an integral part of the community. It was home to countless families who lived and worked there for two or three generations. Some children grew up on the grounds, because their parents were a part of the operations. Cindi Hummer's grandparents, parents and uncle provided over one hundred years of state service. She recalls that it was a close-knit, social community. Her mother worked in the receiving unit for twenty-five years and ran the Imola Broadcasting System, which aired music and news. Her father was a full-time fireman for thirty-eight years. The children played on huge swing sets near the hospital entrance and enjoyed exploring the property, which was their backyard. Every Christmas Day, Santa's sleigh was pulled by the chief's truck around the grounds, with her dad, Vernon Nowlin, dressed as Santa Claus.

In the old days, the patients would take the trolley up Soscol into downtown Napa; the tracks were buried when Highway 29 was built. The only vestige was the Greyhound bus stop across from the gate to the hospital. In 1966, the Fair Labor Standards Act required that state hospitals begin paying patients for their labor. In 1977, occupational therapy was replaced by optional vocational services programs, which paid patients thirty to sixty cents per hour for work that was supplemental to the essential functioning of the facility. Starting in 1967 with cutbacks ordered by Governor Ronald Reagan and in 1968 with the Lanterman-Petris-Short Act, the process of deinstitutionalization began. Napa State Hospital closed its dairy, sold its orchards to Napa Community College and to the City of Napa to create Kennedy Park, in honor of the recently deceased president, and returned

Left: Peter Zwetsloot began working for the state hospital as a psych tech, eventually becoming a supervisor. Later, he worked in the warehouse with a total of twenty-two years of service. *Courtesy of Peter Zwetsloot.*

Right: Phong Vu and his little brother, Cuong. *Courtesy of Phong Vu.*

the land that is now part of Skyline Park to the state. These closures had a huge impact on Napa Valley, as the state hospital had been a major employer.

Community programs funded through counties were supposed to provide support for discharged patients and replace the state hospital model. These changes led to an increase in homelessness and significantly reduced the level of care. Now, the state hospital is a locked facility used only for people in jail judged to be mentally ill. Although its patients are prisoners, the workers are not allowed to carry protection.

But in the 1980s, asylum pears still grew on the Napa College campus. Dr. Phong Vu remembers when his family came to Napa in 1981, sponsored by St. Apollinaris:

> *My father found a temporary job working on the campus. I remember my mother taking my brother and me to the pear orchards. We'd come fully prepared with our brown paper grocery bags and just pick away, sometimes until daylight was gone. After we would take them home, my*

mom would wash them, skin them and cut them into pieces for my brother and me. Although sweet, I remember them being somewhat of a dry texture, not like the ones you would find at the store these days. Oftentimes we had picked so much that the extra pears would eventually make their way to other family households.

FIRE DEPARTMENT AND FIREFIGHTER MUSEUM, DOWNTOWN NAPA

Rita Harren Bordwell wrote a history of the fire department and organized a firefighter museum to preserve that history. Bordwell tells how, in early Napa, before 1859, the only resources to fight fires were wells and pumps: "Women and girls pumped, men passed the buckets." In 1859, the first volunteer fire company was founded; by 1873, the Napa Hook and Ladder Company had been added. Bordwell describes the vaudeville shows held at Napa High to raise funds for the volunteers and the New Year's Balls held at the Opera House, where the Napa Band played until midnight, when attendees broke for refreshments and dancing until 5:00 a.m.

Bordwell writes: "My father [Charles Harren] served between 1884 and 1886. He was injured by a falling burning wall and resigned at the request of Mother—but he never missed a fire as long as he lived. We have a picture of my father in his uniform holding the bugle which was used to call 'the boys' together."

She reports that when there was a fire, "everyone turned out" to watch the friendly competition between the different volunteer fire companies. She praises Henry and Ed Manasse of Sawyer Tannery, whose own firefighting organization, the Reliance Hose Company, "always offered assistance" to the town.

The earliest fire station was located on Brown Street directly across from the courthouse. Finally, in 1907, Napa created its first paid fire department, and a new fire station was built in 1926 on First Street at the site of the old Central School. The fire chief and his family lived on the west side of the building, "the boys" stayed on the east side. The chief's wife organized a sewing club to help the needy, and the fire station opened the first repair shop for children's toys. The crews distributed Christmas trees for the community from the station. The station was demolished when the current Station One was constructed around 1960 on Seminary Street. The building on Brown Street was damaged during the 2014 earthquake and torn down.

Rita Bordwell, about 1930. *Courtesy of Napa County Historical Society.*

Left: This mannequin wears the actual uniform of Napa's first female firefighter, Jane De'Zell, hired in March 1985. *Courtesy of Lauren Coodley*.

Below: Napa firefighters at Fire Station One, located on Second Street between Seminary and Church Street, around 1950. *Courtesy of Napa County Historical Society*.

Captain Bob Foley recalls: "Many of us old-timers knew Rita Bordwell. When I was first hired by the City of Napa in 1965, she used to stop by for a visit with the 'fire laddies.' She always had a story to tell and would remind us that her father was one of the original volunteer firefighters on the Pioneer Engine Company here in Napa in the late 1800s."

Foley remembers how Rita Bordwell organized the museum: "She shamed the guys into getting their photos for us." In her own hand, she inscribed the names of all the firefighters on the backs of the 589 photographs she collected. In the 1940s, the building at 1201 Main Street housed a grocery store, appliance store and auto parts shop. The Firefighters Museum was opened on July 16, 1994, the eighty-eighth birthday of the Napa Fire Department.

The museum closed on November 13, 2014. The property was owned by the Napa Redevelopment Agency and was intended to be developed. When redevelopment agencies were eliminated by the state, all properties were sold. The contents of the museum are stored in an unknown location.

When Carol Bray decided to create a firefighter cookbook, Rita Bordwell was still alive. Carol included Rita's recipe for a lemon angel pie in the book. From this cookbook, which covers 1964 to 1974, one learns about the requirements necessary to become a firefighter (if you were male; the first woman was hired in 1985), how to make a sour cherry pie or how to cut a flank steak. Bray remembered: "When I first went to work for the fire department, I was amazed at the sight of 27 grown men cooking their own meals....The men had a vegetable garden outside the station, until the city in its wisdom chopped down the old peach tree and paved the garden to make still another parking lot."

Bray concludes: "Where else could a person work, get a dozen red roses and big cake from the male chauvinists for your birthday, as well as eight assorted bottles of wine, besides a world of sweet talk, free coffee and an occasional lunch year-round. In those days the men paid ten dollars a month or a dollar a day to eat at the firehouse."

SOUTHERN PACIFIC RAILROAD AND ELECTRIC RAILROADS, CALISTOGA THROUGH VALLEJO

Sam Brannan wanted a railroad to bring his customers. Forests were felled on the hillsides for the wood-burning furnaces on the trains; eucalyptus trees were imported from Australia with the misguided idea of using them for fuel or railroad ties. Brannan recruited Chinese men from the province of Canton to help lay the Napa Valley Railroad (NVRR) and work in the quicksilver mines in Pope Valley. Two miles south of Napa, Vallejo's old Rancho Suscol, which had once been the cone of a submarine volcano, became a quarry for basalt gold rock. Chinese workers set dynamite charges, cleared rubble from shafts and routinely were killed or maimed in mining accidents.

Southern Pacific Railroad train, Oakville, late 1880s. *Courtesy of Napa County Historical Society.*

The first engine, called the Calistoga, arrived in Napa in 1865. When the switching yard for the trains was constructed in American Canyon, it was named Napa Junction. Only a few miles from the first naval base on the Pacific Coast (Mare Island), trains were switched for Solano, Sacramento, Sonoma, Marin and the East Bay.

A traveler could board the train at Suscol and get off at Thompson Station, the Napa Depot at Suscol and Fourth Street or the West Napa Depot on California Street. Service to Calistoga was completed by 1868. California Pacific purchased the NVRR in 1869; Southern Pacific bought Cal-Pacific in 1885 and operated passenger service to Calistoga until 1929. In 1885, the Southern Pacific Railroad Company purchased the line and operated it for the next 102 years.

Napa also had an electric railroad, completed in 1905. Napa's mayor, J.A. Fuller, announced, "Napa for half a century has been slumbering in a Rip Van Winkle sleep but she has awakened at last." A great banquet was held by The 20,000 Club of Vallejo to celebrate the link between the Vallejo ferry and the railroad, which was located next to the ferry building. The first chartered electric train carried fifty-five officers and sailors from Mare Island to Napa, along with "several ladies and a ten piece band." The band gave a public concert at the Napa courthouse. By 1907, the Napa-Vallejo and Benicia Railroad offered a special round trip for Vallejo

Top: Napa Canning Company before it burned down, East Napa. *Bottom*: Napa Valley Railroad electric train at the depot in 1906. *Courtesy of Napa County Historical Society.*

women who worked at the canning company in East Napa; tickets were fifteen cents.

In 1929, the Southern Pacific shut down its Napa passenger line, cut river service from South Vallejo to Napa Junction and turned over mail delivery to the electric railroad. In 1930, Greyhound Bus Lines sought permission from the California Railroad Commission to merge its companies in California to compete with the railroads. The Napa City Council, the Napa Chamber of Commerce and the Napa Central Labor Council opposed the expansion of Greyhound. They believed that the interurban "had long rendered adequate, dependable, and comfortable transportation service," writes Ira Swett, railroad historian.

In 1932, a fire erupted in Napa's electric train barn. Cars were destroyed, the expensive electrical equipment was incinerated and the railway seemed done. Manager Clyde Brown had to lay off all seventy employees, but townspeople came to the support of the interurban, aggressively campaigning to get the big trains back in service. Feature ads were purchased in the newspapers calling for electric railway service to resume. None of these efforts saved the railway, and by 1938, buses had successfully replaced the electric train. People no longer traveled from the East Bay or San Francisco by ferry to Vallejo and onto the electric train to Napa. Mary Campbell recalls:

> *My father Frank C. Olsen was the Signal Maintainer for the Southern Pacific Railroad for the Napa District, which stretched from Vallejo to Suisun, Sonoma, and Calistoga. We moved to Napa in June of 1947 and lived in the company house on 801 Eighth Street until July of 1960. My father was the last Signal Maintainer to live in the house with his family.*
>
> *Our neighbor was George Blaufuss, owner of Saxon Apple Cider, at the corner of Soscol and Eighth Street. Across the tracks was the Basalt Rock headquarters, and on the other corner was the Union Ice company and lockers.*
>
> *Whenever the steam locomotives would sit on the tracks, the engine was kept running and the steam vapor would condense and run down the street. And also the hobos who would arrive each Spring looking for work in the valley. One was named T-Bone Riley who returned over the years. Some*

Southern Pacific Railroad Signal Maintainers home. *Courtesy of Mary Campbell.*

hobos had carved their names on my dad's work shed, with some names going back to the 1920s.

In 1987, the Southern Pacific railroad was sold to the Napa Valley Wine Train Inc. The new owner refurbished the cars to give visitors an opportunity to experience the romance of the past by cruising through the valley. Napans still get to listen to the sound of the train whistle in our imaginations.

SAWYER TANNERY, SOUTH COOMBS STREET

In the late nineteenth century, seven wharves were constructed along the Napa waterfront, along with lumberyards and warehouses. Steamers carried both agricultural and industrial products, sometimes transporting entire flocks and herds of livestock to Napa docks. French Albert Sawyer from New Hampshire was visiting Napa when he noticed that local butchers were discarding sheep pelts with wool still on them. He purchased a pile of those pelts and started a wool-pulling business on the banks of the Napa River, aided by Chinese laborers. Soon, he was curing hides, pickling them in brine and shipping them back East.

In 1870, he founded the Sawyer Tanning Company on South Coombs Street. A year later, French invited Emmanuel Manasse, a German immigrant who was running a successful tannery in the Mission District of San Francisco, to move with his family to Napa to work for him. He joined the company and rapidly developed new methods for tanning sheepskin and buckskin.

In 1900, the tannery was buying deerskins for thirty-eight cents a pound in the summer; in winter, for twenty-eight cents. Wet, salted cowhides cost nine cents a pound; horsehides cost two dollars. By 1909, Sawyer Tannery had developed Napatan Waterproof Leather and Napa Patent Leather and Emanuel Manasse became co-owner of the business. In 1917, Emanuel's son Henry Manasse opened a shoe store downtown and built a family home at 845 Jefferson Street. When the supply demands of World War I caused a shortage of chemicals, Sawyer sent engineers and miners into the surrounding hills and found chrome ore to make dichromate of soda, the chemical essential to tanning.

By the 1920s, Sawyer was the first tannery west of Chicago to produce patent leather. In 1927, it developed chromed tan leather (the ideal material for fashioning softball gloves) and, later, leather for baseball and welding gloves. In the twenties and thirties, the South Franklin neighborhood, a

Workers at Sawyer Tannery include Ah Chong, Chas Philips, Joe Ezettie, Robert Thompson, Wilson brothers, Louie Cassayre Ezettie, August Manasse, George Thompson and Louis Banchero, 1899. *Courtesy of Napa County Historical Society.*

Fiftieth-anniversary celebration of Sawyer Tannery in 1919. *Courtesy of Napa County Historical Society.*

Sawyer color wheel workers. Sharon Arnold's father, Chester van Gorder, is the dark-haired man on the right. "He went in at 7:00 and worked until everything was done and many days that was early afternoon so he would fish the Napa River." *Courtesy of Napa County Historical Society.*

couple of blocks from the tannery, was home to tanners, paper hangers, stevedores, rivermen and their families.

Even during the Depression, Sawyer Tannery continued to thrive, turning out woolen lining for coats and all kinds of gloves. The tannery offered hard work, sometimes dangerous and always involving exposure to the toxic materials used to tan hides. But a man could make a living with his hands throughout most of the twentieth century.

Peter Manasse is the great-grandson of Emanuel Manasse, who came up to Napa on horse and buggy "and said, look I can tan those things." He went to work for Sawyer and became a partner almost immediately. Emanuel's first house, built in 1886, was at 443 Brown Street, south of Oak. It was known as the Manasse Mansion until five years ago, when it was renamed the Violet Mansion, now Historic Landmark No. 78000723.

After Emanuel Manasse joined the Sawyer company, he rapidly developed new methods for tanning sheepskin and buckskin. Emanuel's other sons were Ed and August. Both began working at Sawyer, but Ed

Sawyer Tannery workers, mid-twentieth century. *Courtesy of Napa County Historical Society.*

stayed with the company. August founded a tannery in Berkeley, Manasse Block Tannery. Irving went to work at Sawyer's, along with his brothers, and later founded his own tannery, CalNap, next door, in 1945, the year after his father's death. The Edward Manasse House at 495 Coombs Street is also a Registered Historic Landmark (No. 93000271). Ray Guadagni recalls:

As a teen, I visited a friend of mine, Sal Garcia, who worked at CalNap. It seemed so dangerous to me. Sal's job was to put hides into a vat of horribly toxic stuff and stir it. He had to wear rubber gloves that went up to his shoulders and an apron and goggles, but there were still parts of his face and neck that were exposed to this acid should a splash occur from stirring too vigorously. It didn't seem to me that the job was worth the $1.25 per hour they were paying him, pre-OSHA.

Peter Manasse remembers the "whistle blowing every day at 7 and 1 and 4," the chemicals and dissolved hair being tossed into the Napa River, while the fleshings went to a tallow company. He remembers the barges coming up the river bringing diesel fuel for their boiler, and the hides arriving by freight train. He remembers driving a big flatbed truck across the Third Street Bridge to pick up the hides at the train depot at Fourth and Soscol. Sawyer Tannery was such a major employer that "most people did work at the tannery in high school or grammar school." Napa was so small that "if I drove my parents' car too fast downtown, a police officer would call them." Peter became the manager of Tulocay Cemetery in 1989 after sorrowfully closing Cal-Nap: "I know more people out at the cemetery than I know in the town of Napa," he said. Sawyer Tannery gave final notice to its employees in 1990. Parts of the old building are now an arts center, and the tower remains.

CAMERON SHIRT COMPANY, OAK STREET

The Cameron Shirt Company, which opened in 1901, became the first union shop in town, its workforce turning out twelve hundred work shirts in a day. W.H. Cameron, a salesman for Levi Strauss in San Francisco, founded the company and brought a young cutter named Bert Gans to act as superintendent in 1901. Rita Bordwell comments, "I don't believe there ever was any superintendent that was as popular as Bert Gans. San Francisco requested his help to affiliate with the Shirtmakers Union. All joined, at the request of Messrs. Cameron and Gans."

Carl Franco's father, John Franco, was born in Argentina. John came to America as an indentured servant and worked grafting trees in the Napa orchards. Carl's mother, Amelia Banchero, was descended from a pioneer Napa family who had emigrated from Italy in 1875 and bought land on Soda Springs Road. Her father, Louie, worked at Sawyer Tannery. The family home was on Eggleston Street. Carl Franco was born in California

EXIT

Opposite, top: The Cameron Shirt Factory, 1953, with mother of Wendy Beltrami, Gail Randol (*in the back on the right*), who worked in payroll. *Courtesy of Wendy Beltrami.*

Opposite, bottom: Franco family photo. *Courtesy of Les Franco.*

Above: Franco family wedding photo. *Courtesy of Les Franco.*

in 1910. According to the 1930 census, Carl Franco was the head of the household's son, twenty years old and identified as white and unmarried.

Upon graduation from Napa High, Carl Franco attended Heald Business College in Oakland and then was hired by Cameron Shirt Company. In 1945, Carl was president of Local 137 of the Garment Workers Union. He was in the cutting room at the time of his death in 1946, at thirty-six years old. "Local Union No. 137 mourns death of Carl Franco" was the headline story on April 5, 1946, in the *Garment Worker*. The Garment Workers obituary reveals that Franco was a member of the Young Men's Institute, Knights of Dunamis, Audubon Club and Saint John's Church Choir and was the assistant scout leader of Troop No. 10. More than one hundred Scouts formed a guard of honor at the church, and Cameron Shirt Company closed its doors during the funeral. The Cameron Shirt Factory became part of Rough Rider in 1955.

THE CCC CAMP, LAS POSADAS FOREST, ANGWIN

During the 1930s, the Roosevelt administration and Congress created the New Deal to lift America up from the Great Depression. The New Deal consisted of dozens of new programs and policies that addressed the nation's pressing needs: infrastructure, environmental conservation, wage growth, retirement benefits, healthcare, child care, affordable housing and farm pricing. New Deal historian Brent McKee explains:

> *One of the largest of the New Deal programs, the Works Progress Administration, employed 8.5 million jobless Americans on public works of all kinds, including 650,000 miles of roadwork, tens of thousands of artworks for public places, and 1.2 billion school lunches served to children. We're still using many WPA projects today: crossing WPA bridges, drinking from WPA water lines, using WPA-collected history materials to research our family histories.*

The WPA completed what local newspapers referred to as "extensive" roadwork throughout the county and also worked on the Napa water storage plant at Lake Milliken. Between 1935 and 1940, WPA workers in Napa County built or improved thirty-two miles of roads, thirteen public buildings, a grandstand, a sewage treatment plant, 155 culverts and more. Also, thirteen hundred acres were drained for mosquito control, many

Civilian Conservations Corps workers, California. *Courtesy of the National Archives.*

miles of new fire and forest trails were built, 3,579 feet of retaining walls and revetments were constructed and reconstructed and fourteen hundred square yards of surface were riprapped, with construction or modernization of nearly five miles of water mains and distribution lines.

A Civilian Conservation Corps (CCC) camp was established at Las Posadas in 1933. The *St. Helena Star* reported:

> *The company had no sooner established itself than part of the men were called out to fight a fire in the hills east of Napa. Besides fire fighting, when necessary, the men will be employed building fire trails, building roads and other improvements.... The men are given every opportunity to improve their minds during their stay at camp. Evening classes in languages, mathematics and other subjects for which there is a call are to be given in the recreation room....At present the meals are served at the 4-H camp, pending the completion of the mess hall.*

Jeff Johnson's father, Ken, "signed up for several programs during the early FDR, New Deal administration to help earn extra money, eventually arriving in California during the Great Depression, finding work in the CCC. This new work in California continued his education."

Shortly after the CCC left, unemployed men were hired by the WPA to reopen the camp facilities and continue some of their forestry work. Following the close of the CCC program in 1942, the old camp was used as a forestry camp and rebuilt as a California Department of Forestry and Fire Protection (CAL FIRE) fire station in the early 1950s.

In 1959, a local paper praised the CCC's work: "One of the most important achievements of the total conservation crew is the road which they built to the top of Mt. St. Helena, and the lookout they established there which has become the area's most important check-spot for fires."

ROUGH RIDER ON SOSCOL

In 1936, the Napa Chamber of Commerce made a proposal to Rough Rider Clothing Factory of San Francisco: if the factory moved to Napa, the chamber would raise and donate the $40,000 needed to buy the land, a lot between the river and the train tracks, on Soscol, half a mile south of Third Street. Before the Rough Rider plant was built, the site at Sixth and Soscol had been used for the manufacture of windmills, beer and shoes. Julian Weidler, who had worked for Rough Rider while he attended college in Berkeley, was sent to Napa to set up the factory. There were many men's clothing stores in downtown Napa eager for Rough Rider apparel, including Voorhees, Straus, Albert's and Grossman's. After Rough Rider opened, boats from Lowell, Massachusetts, carried cotton and wool through the Panama Canal into the San Francisco Bay and up the Napa River on barges to unload at the factory. Rough Rider also transported materials on the Southern Pacific, whose railroad depot was across the street.

While boys graduating from Napa High could count on becoming union apprentices at Mare Island, girls did not have similar job opportunities. When Rough Rider came to town, Napa High began offering girls training in industrial sewing; eventually, over five hundred workers, mostly women, went on to employment at Rough Rider. Weidler recalls that he always had cordial relations with his unionized employees.

The Rough Rider Cookbook was published by the United Garment Workers. Along with recipes, this cookbook offers a list of unionized occupations in Napa, including bartenders, retail clerks, musicians, dried-fruit packers, barbers, cleaners, carpet layers and grain processors.

Rough Rider employee. *Courtesy of Napa County Historical Society.*

Rough Rider Clothing Factory extended generous amounts of credit to its Bay Area customers, who still remember that they were saved from economic disaster during the Depression. Rita Bordwell recorded her memories of the rise of unions in Napa:

> *A friend of mine, a member of a union, rang me up one day and asked me if I would be interested in a position as secretary to the new business manager that the Central Labor and Building Trades expected to hire. He took me to the Labor Temple to meet them: Otis Brown, Carpenters; Earl McCall, Laborers; Earl Mack, Painters, Will O'Keefe, Plumbers, Will Gellinger, Lathers; Bob Findley, Electricians; and Washington Mannering, Garment Workers.*

In 1938, this group hired George Bobst, who had been a labor leader in both San Francisco and Vallejo, as its business manager. Bordwell recalled that the first union office was on Pearl Street, behind the Napa City Bakery. Bobst realized that larger quarters were needed. He surveyed

The Lazarus Auto Supply auto workers union meeting in the mid-late 1930s, with Wendy Beltrami's grandfather, Sam Gardner *(fourth from right)*. *Courtesy of Wendy Beltrami.*

Site of the former Labor Temple, Main Street, Napa. *Courtesy of Lauren Coodley.*

the town and found the Prohibition Hall at Main and Vallejo Streets. The Carpenters Union, which had the most funds at the time, purchased the building; later, the other unions paid their share. The labor temple on Main Street is now a real estate office.

In 1970, Rough Rider was still one of the four largest private industries in the valley, employing more than seven hundred people. Barry Nelson recalls: "My dad and grandma worked there! I used to go visit my dad and was amazed at the process—he was a cutter—cut scraps of fabric into a pattern, which was then sent over to the gals on the sewing machine."

By 1980, however, Rough Rider had closed its Napa operations entirely due mainly to free trade laws that allowed corporations to seek the lowest-paid workers abroad. Maria Brambila recalls: "I began working at the garment factory Rough Rider, and then it was bought out by the Koret Company. I worked at this company for almost ten years, until the Koret Company went out of business."

After Rough Rider, the structure accommodated a manufacturer of horse blankets, a bird specialty store and an antiques emporium. The

Governor Ronald Reagan with Mr. Weidler during his 1970 visit. *Courtesy of Julian Weidler.*

Rough Rider building was leveled in August 2002. Kevin Courtney wrote:

> *The flood control project is razing the former clothing factory so the eastern bank of the Napa River can be widened with marsh and floodplain terraces that will come up almost to Soscol…."It's great for us," said Nancy Lochmann, general manager for the Napa River Inn and Hatt Market on the west bank of the river. "This will be the first time that anybody has been able to see us."*

The river project paid $4.1 million to acquire the Rough Rider property for demolition. Engineered Demolition Inc. of Coeur d'Alene, Idaho, brought the building down. The company also removed the former Shrimp Boat restaurant near Imola and the Ice House on Soscol.

BASALT AND KAISER, SOUTH OF NAPA CITY

Basalt Rock, which had already built its first barge for the navy in July 1940, built a complete shipyard on its property, with four dry docks to provide ship maintenance. Harold Halterman, retired plant manager, told Kevin Courtney: "The war was coming on. Mr. Streblow saw this opportunity. The Navy needed barges out in the Pacific." Lorraine Kongsgaard, Streblow's daughter, recalls: "People used to say, why did you build this shipyard in a hayfield? He'd say, 'Because it's home.'" Basalt was located south of Imola and the State Hospital, alongside what became the Napa Vallejo Highway, on the east side of the road.

The inaugural issue of the shipyard newspaper, the *Basalt Beacon*, announced: "Surmounting obstacles that at times appeared impossible, Basalt Rock Company has answered this great Nation's call for implements of war." As Courtney writes: "Soon, three thousand workers from Texas, Oklahoma, and a dozen other hardscrabble places were working around the clock on ships as long as football fields." Attillio "Tilly" Musante put in forty-seven years at Basalt Rock. "We were just a bunch of prune-pickers," he said. "We didn't know nothing." During the war, Musante etched the designs into the wood flooring of the mold loft. From these etchings, patterns were made and steel cut.

Basalt launched two U.S. Navy tankers onto the Napa River, the USS *Crownblock* and the USS *Whipstock*, and received the U.S. Army-Navy E

Basalt shipyard, Napa. *Courtesy of Napa County Historical Society.*

Swede Johnson at home on Spencer Street, 2006. *Courtesy of Lauren Coodley.*

Aerial photo of Kaiser Steel. *Courtesy of Napa County Historical Society.*

Award in recognition of an outstanding production record. Obediah "Swede" Johnson, who worked as a quicksilver miner in Lake County before the war, came to Basalt in 1942. He told Kevin Courtney: "I had never seen a ship, except in pictures maybe....The union made the blue collar people powerful. I don't think we'd have a pension plan without one." Rita Bordwell remembers, "there were more jobs than workers" after the war began. In 1943, workers enjoyed the first Labor Day celebration on the site. Two thousand men and women marched in the parade, barbecued in the afternoon and danced all night at the fairgrounds.

Rita Bordwell describes Kaiser Steel Shipyard coming to Napa in 1955, when the company purchased the Basalt plant site and expanded and upgraded it. "We [the union] took charge of all the metal crafts[men] who would be employed there." A large assembly bay was added to the plate shop in 1956, and two years later, a second finishing line was added to the pipe mill, giving it the largest production capacity for such pipe in the United States. Many workers began their careers with Basalt and retired from Kaiser, never working for any other employer. Thurman Mount was one of these men. He lived in Shipyard Acres while his father worked at the adjacent Basalt Shipyard. When Thurman turned eighteen in 1947, he signed on as a machinist's helper and stayed for forty-eight years. "I had my best years out there with Kaiser Steel.... We were just a happy bunch of people. We made jokes with each other."

One by one, factories in Napa disappeared, Kaiser Steel closing its doors in 1983. With the clanging of the great doors, the leveling of the buildings and the transition of blue-collar workplaces to art galleries and tourist centers, scores of workers were displaced and young high school graduates lost the opportunity to work at manufacturing jobs.

WORKING AT THE *NAPA REGISTER*, DOWNTOWN NAPA

The Old Napa Register Building, at 1202 First Street, was built in 1905. The *Register*, founded in 1863 as a weekly, began daily publication in 1872. George Milton Francis became sole owner and publisher in 1876 and ran it until the 1920s, when his son George R. Francis took over. Francis bought property at Coombs and First Streets in 1904, and the newspaper office was designed by architect L.M. Turton. In early years, the second floor was leased as a dance studio.

Reporter Phyllis King was one of the few female journalists who kept her job after World War II. Phyllis, born in 1924, graduated from Napa

Napa Register Building, 1906, where Phyllis King worked. *Courtesy of Napa County Historical Society.*

High in 1942, attended Stanford, then moved to Marysville and worked on a daily paper during World War II. King's daughter Liz Reyna writes of her mother:

> *After my mother separated from my dad, she moved back to Napa. We moved to downtown Napa, where we lived in an old Victorian on Second Street. This is where most of my mom's newspaper career took place. She was a versatile reporter, covering everything from what was then called "women's news" to politics, major news stories, travel, and scientific advances. She had a terrific sense of humor, a very quick mind, knew everyone in town, and was a very social person. She had reddish brown hair, gorgeous and naturally wavy, was always slim and enjoyed up-to-date styles.*

Reyna describes how her mother simultaneously worked in a "man's world" and also managed to "wallpaper several tall rooms in her old Victorian with only the help of two young children." Phyllis King would sit at her typewriter, either at home or at the *Napa Register* office, with the phone cradled on her shoulder, getting information on some breaking

Phyllis King with her colleagues at the *Napa Register*. *Courtesy of Liz Reyna.*

news and pounding away at her keyboard at the same time: "Within moments the story would roll out of the typewriter, a finished product requiring only minor edits before it would appear in the next day's paper. She worked a full day at the *Register*, and then came home to write Napa stories for the *Sacramento Bee* and the *Oakland Tribune*. By 9:00 p.m., we would drive down to the bus depot to send the stories off for the morning's editions."

Phyllis King herself gives a vivid account of what it was like to work for a local paper in the forties. She describes working with *Register* editor Arthur MacKay "in the days when reporters used folded over half sheets of copy paper to be held easily in the left hand...before they donned horned rimmed glasses and bought clipboards." Mac's predecessor was George Peck.

Phyllis King's writing transports us to old Napa, where people gathered downtown at the Plaza Hotel Bar. It was a time when everyone read the daily newspaper, which held those thirteen thousand souls together in community—the world that she chronicled with such delight.

The *Napa Register* moved to 1615 Second Street in 1966. After the earthquake destroyed the Second Street offices in 2014, the *Register* moved to 1615 Soscol Avenue. The original building, the Beckstoffer Building, was listed in the National Register of Historic Places in 1982. Now, there is a retail store with leather goods called Overland Sheepskin Store.

YOUNTVILLE SCHOOL AND WILDA ADDIS

Wilda Addis, a legendary Yountville teacher, began her career at Yountville Grammar School in 1923. For over forty years, she maintained strict classroom discipline as she educated several generations of Yountville children. Muriel Callison, Wilda Addis's friend and coworker, began the first hot-lunch program at Yountville Grammar School in 1933. She fed countless Yountville children for thirty years without missing a day. The Yountville School was closed by the Napa School District in 2020.

Wilda Addis posing with Muriel Callison during her retirement party in 1967. The cake, baked by Muriel, was in the shape of the Yountville School. *Courtesy of John Callison.*

4

WHERE WE PLAYED

Play is something done for its own sake.... It's voluntary, it's pleasurable, it offers a sense of engagement, it takes you out of time. And the act itself is more important than the outcome.

—Dr. Stuart Brown, *Play*

SKATING RINKS, NAPA

In 1882, Captain Albert Hatt purchased land at the corner of Brown and Fourth Streets from Napa founder William H. Coombs for just one dollar. The Hatt Buildings and the Napa Mill Complex, constructed between 1884 and 1887, are Napa's oldest large brick industrial buildings made from Napa River clay. From a young age, Hatt lived the life of a seafarer, eventually becoming a boat captain on the Sacramento River. He settled in Napa and in 1884 began construction on the Hatt Buildings, from which he sold coal, grain and vegetables. They are two closely linked large warehouses built of native brick. Beyond being a cornerstone of Napa's commercial industries, the Hatt complex was also a center for community activity.

The Hatt Buildings included a second story, complete with a skating rink. A year later, in 1885, the captain improved the rink with a new floor of tongue-and-groove planking made of white rock maple shipped from Chicago. Later, 50 pairs of new nickel-plated clamp skates were added to the 165 pairs already available at the rink. Many Napans enjoyed frequent social events at the Hatt skating rink. The *Napa Register* of February 13, 1885, describes one such event:

The Hatt Building, Napa. *Courtesy of River Inn.*

> *The obstacle race at Cleveland's* [the rink's manager] *rink last Saturday evening was attended by a large gathering and the entertainment which the race afforded was rich, rare and racy. The skaters were required to crawl through barrels, climb over ropes and scantlings and walk between the rounds of ladders laid flat upon the floor. The audience roared itself hoarse with laughter at the hasty and ludicrous gyrations of the racers.*

The elder Hatt died in 1913, and his warehouse holdings were sold to the Keig family. The Keigs established Napa Milling, which produced agricultural feed and sold farm supplies and developed vegetarian feed and mash products for Napa County's sizable Seventh-day Adventist community. The Mill closed in 1974, ushering in a long period of vacancy. Though placed in the National Register of Historic Places in 1979, the fate of the Hatt/Mill complex was uncertain for many years. Renovation led by Harry Price began in 1992. The remodel sought to preserve many of the historic features of the building, such as the silo towering above Napa's waterfront and the milling equipment that can be found in Sweetie Pies bakery. Elegant tinwork and flooring can be found in Hatt Hall and many of the Napa River Inn's hotel rooms as well. Today, the hotel rooms located on the second floor of the main building of the Napa River Inn feature the original rock maple wood plank flooring on which revelers skated, danced and even dribbled in years past.

The next rink was opened on Juarez Street in the 1940s. It was run by the Fournier family and was open through the early to mid-sixties. The rink sponsored competitions, with prizes for the most graceful skaters. Rhonda Torres recalls, "Many a summer afternoon was spent on that old wooden floor." Marlene Wilson Hurley remembers: "It was nice because there was a mixed crowd of young, younger, older, etc. It was an acceptable place for groups of girls and boys to go with maybe one adult in the background. We could skate afternoons and it seems there was evenings too. The music was fun also. Rental shoes were affordable as well. Saturdays were popular too."

The rink was at the location of the old recycling center on First Street. The site of the skating rink became the Furniture 4 Less store and still had the original wood floors throughout the building. The structure was torn down after the 2014 earthquake, when Furniture 4 Less moved out.

The next—and last—skating rink was at River Park Shopping Center. Called the Wheelhouse Rink, it was owned and operated by the Duckworth family from 1978 to 1988. Carl Nicholson writes: "It was important to me as well growing up. I lived there practically....I was on the speed skating team and a Wheelhouse club member. Good times." Judy Harrison adds:

> *We were all crying when it closed down....I got a call from my BFF Tracey Kite about them bulldozing the whole building. I just cried because that whole building was only meant to be a skating rink. I just watched that when all these skating rinks were open the crime rates were very low everywhere in the USA and as they keep closing them down the crime rates are rising fast. This is because kids have some places to go and the parents are happy these kids are in a safe zone. When Wheelhouse closed down, I started ditching school and I started smoking and drinking and just hanging in the streets because there wasn't ANYTHING I COULD DO.*

CIRCUSES AT THE FAIRGROUNDS

Once a year, the circus came to town. The Depot was at Fourth and Soscol. The circus train would enter town on the tracks of the Napa Valley Railroad (NVRR), built in 1864 from the head of navigation (farthest point above the head of a river that can be navigated by ships) in the Napa River. The route ran from Skaggs Island all the way to Calistoga. Freight trains would continue their runs into the 1980s.

In 1930, Dave Cavagnaro organized the first Italian-Catholic Federation convention, the firefighter parade and the "Circus Fans" organization. Cavagnaro, son of Italian immigrants, had arrived in Napa as a baby in 1883 and been fascinated with what he could see, hear and smell of the circus ever since Al Barnes and the elephants paraded past his front door in 1918. Al's elephant parade included ten Asian elephants, among them the bulls Tusko, Black Diamond and Vance. Andrew Clerici remembers: "I used to go to the Depot in the morning and wait for the train. They would unload and set up for the 2 o'clock show and then another show in the evening. They had a little parade of animals through town about noon to advertise that they were there. By eight in the morning they were gone...everything was clean and you could not tell they had ever been here."

Dave Cavagnaro and his wife, Nellie, continued to operate the Brooklyn Hotel at Third and Soscol, the gathering place for the Italian American community. Dave tended bar, sang and played his concertina. He, Nellie and kids Anita, Ray and Robert lived upstairs; they rented rooms to single Italian men working on the railroad. On April 18, 1935, Dave hosted a dinner at his hotel for thirty-five performers from the Tom Mix Circus and Wild West Show.

Cavagnaro decided to set aside twelve weeks of every year to travel with either Ringling Brothers or the Clyde Beatty Circus. Martin Mini writes this about this family member: "He pitched hay, ran errands, helped in the front office, sold tickets, collected tickets, unloaded animals, set up and tore down tents, carried water to the animals...acted as a booking agent, functioned as an advance man and a roustabout."

Jeff Johnson remembers how, when Barnum & Bailey set up its circus at the Napa Fairgrounds: "For a kid my age, just hearing about it was amazing. To add to our enjoyment, Dad took us downtown to see elephants help hoist the huge tent poles followed by a wonderful oatmeal and brown sugar breakfast back home on Brown Street."

Left: Dave Cavagnaro leading a parade on horseback. *Courtesy of Napa County Historical Society.*

Below: Ad for the Napa Fair in *Napa County Record*, August 5, 1959. *Courtesy of Napa County Historical Society.*

Mary Campbell recalls: "What I remember most clearly was the Clyde Beatty Circus that would pass through Napa every summer on the rails, and then it would unload its circus animals across from the Union Ice Company office on Soscol Avenue. The various animals—elephants, horses, etc.—would be offloaded and then guided across Soscol Avenue to the fairgrounds where their circus tent would be put up."

In 1955, Cathy Mathews was six years old, and her mother, Lucille, brought her to see the Clyde Beatty Circus at the Napa Fairgrounds. Cathy remembers: "The smells of sawdust, peanuts and popcorn. The trapeze artists came out in those big showy costumes—I was very impressed. Clyde Beatty had this whip that he snapped in the air at the lions and tigers."

Circuses like Ringling Brothers and Clyde Beatty no longer travel the roads, and the long-vanished trains no longer show up in small towns to delight and amaze. Clyde Beatty Circus closed in 1965; Ringling Brothers, under pressure from animal activists, closed in 2017.

THE DREAM BOWL

The Dream Bowl was a large dancehall and concert space. It was the idea of friends Gene Traverso and John Zanardi. They bought the property from the Greenwood family: that name can still be seen on the sign of Greenwood Road, which intersects with South Kelly Road near Highway 12. Michael Amen writes:

> *With family help, they pooled their resources, took a risk, and the construction of the Dream Bowl began. It was scheduled to open in December of 1941—on December 7th as it turned out—but because of the bombing on Pearl Harbor, its opening was delayed....My mother tells me that during World War II, couples were looking for some romantic way to spend their time because it could very well be their last time together.*

The field in which the Dream Bowl stood was off Highway 29 near the Napa Airport, roughly midway between Napa and Vallejo, and was once the largest ballroom in Northern California. The building with its arched roof and great size resembled an airplane hangar. On top of the arched roof and centrally located was a marquee; near Highway 29, on

Mug advertising Dream Bowl. *Courtesy of Michael Amen.*

the outskirts of the property, was a large neon sign advertising at various times snack bars, the H&H Cafe and a regular bar. Dave Cavagnaro's son Bob worked as a liquor distributor for Cavagnaro and Sons. During World War II, he ran the bar at the Dream Bowl, where there were twenty-four-hour-a-day dances in shifts to accommodate the Mare Island workers.

The size of its maple hardwood floor (70 feet wide by 140 feet long) made the nightclub, when it opened, the largest in Northern California. Chris Aultman remembers: "All our parents used to go there." Patsy Cline and Johnny Cash sang at the Dream Bowl.

When Michael Amen recalls when he saw an ad in the *Napa Register* for a concert by the Grateful Dead at the Dream Bowl in 1969: "I was totally captivated....I feel lucky that I got there at that particular nick in time." The building itself still stands, housing Caltest, a specialized commercial environmental analytical chemistry lab focusing on analyses of regulated pollutants at low levels in water.

COMMUNITY CENTER, YOUNT AND MAIN STREETS, NAPA

A group of Napans got together in the late 1930s with the intent of creating a recreation program, but they had no cash. The Works Progress Administration funded and supervised a program in 1941 and may also have funded the construction of the community center itself. In 1941, the *Napa Journal* reported, "The recreation project aided in the formation of the City Basketball league and opened a Community Center at Main and Yount Streets for both adults and children."

This program offered softball, football, basketball, camping trips, playground activities, bicycle races, tap dancing, handicraft classes for children and adults, sketching classes, kite making and model airplane building. Brent McKee of the Living New Deal, whose mission is research, presentation and education, explains:

> *It seems to have existed just that one year, and had a blizzard of well-attended activities. The newspaper archives are just loaded with Napa / WPA recreation events. By 1943 Napans decided to create a recreation program. Napa's present-day recreation program/office is a direct descendant of the WPA recreation program.*

Marlene Wilson Hurley remembers that by the early sixties: "There was an awesome summer recreation program for kids thru high school age who wanted to participate. My group had a college girl, who I think was going to be a teacher. She decided we'd decorate the float for the fair parade. We stuck hundreds of paper napkins thru chicken wire around the entire base of a dump truck. It may have been a small barge. It took forever."

The Napa Recreation Commission became Parks & Recreation in 2000. In 2020, the city proposed eliminating the program, but citizen pressure was successful in saving it.

UPTOWN THEATRE, DOWNTOWN NAPA

Thomas C. Malloy Jr. ran one of the main movie palaces in Napa. He was born in town in 1911. Due to fear of the 1918–20 influenza epidemic, he and his brother were kept out of school and tutored at home until the fourth grade, when they entered Salvador School. Malloy remembered sitting in Dr. C.H. Farman's dental office on the southwest corner of First and Randolph in 1920, watching the construction of the Hippodrome, which became the Fox Theatre. It seated fifteen hundred people and boasted an orchestra pit with a massive pipe organ. Malloy described hearing organist Eugene Brown play during silent movies: "I thought he almost made the organ talk." He continued: "One of my first memories of going to a movie was of my father taking me there, as I recall at my insistence, to see one of Jack Dempsey's early Championship Fight films."

Malloy's first job was in 1930 at the new five-hundred-seat State Theatre on 834 Main Street between Second and Third (now part of Veteran's Park). By 1935, Malloy had become the manager of the Fox, which showed major films and sometimes live presentations.

Above: Fox Theatre was open from 1928 to the late 1940s on the northeast corner of First and Randolph. *Courtesy of Tom Malloy*.

Left: Ad for a movie shown at the Uptown. *Courtesy of Tom Malloy*.

In a grand fashion, the Uptown Theatre opened in August 1937, complete with searchlights, banners and movie stars. Thomas Malloy was its manager. The theater had twelve hundred seats and featured a central ceiling of angels painted by muralist Dick Echeles. Malloy describes the "well-trained team of young ladies in matching uniforms" who served as usherettes. When the house was full, Malloy assigned an usher to every exit and was considered a "safety guy." The *Napa Daily Journal* of August 12, 1937, notes, "a staff of 14 trained theater people have been engaged to serve patrons of the magnificent new Uptown Theatre."

Matinees attracted children like Bob Northrop, who recalls that on Saturday afternoon "every child's bike was parked unlocked at either the Fox or the Uptown." Beautician Chris Aultman especially remembers the mezzanine at the Fox: "I liked going up both sides, it reminded you of something really elegant. Napa was a country town, this was something really special." The film companies would mail in a two-hour film that included a comic and a newsreel.

To survive during the Depression, theater owners devised gimmicks to persuade the public to pay the 35¢ admission price. The most popular promotion was Bank Night, which offered a cash jackpot. A cashier named Dolly handled bank night registration. Malloy remembered: "She was so

Last home of Thomas Malloy, Spruce Street. *Courtesy of Lauren Coodley.*

good at it. I think I fell in love with Dolly from admiration." In 1940, they were married and they bought a house at the corner of Yajome and K Streets for $2,000 with Liberty Head Nickels they saved.

By 1942, air raid rules and blackout procedures had been developed for the town. Malloy recalls: "After Pearl was bombed it was a wild time here. The manning of Monticello Road as a look-out, the presence of Mare Island, made Napans uneasy about being a potential enemy target. It was trying times, and people were looking for an outlet, to get away from things. So they went to the movies." Because one-fifth of the twenty-five thousand workers at Mare Island lived in Napa, special morning matinees were scheduled for swing-shift Mare Island and Basalt workers. They had sing-alongs. Peggy Aaron writes, "I think I remember singing to 'Shine On, Harvest Moon.'"

Between 1947 and 1957, 90 percent of Americans bought television sets. No one realized that supplying screens for home use signaled the beginning of the end for most movie theaters. After the advent of television, Malloy explained, "the majestic Fox was converted into a bowling alley. After a fire ravaged the structure, it was demolished in 1962."

The Uptown Theatre was shuttered until 2000, when George Altamura and partners took ownership and began a massive renovation project to turn the old movie theater into a live music venue. Malloy was invited by George Altamura to consult on the restoration of the Uptown project. He proudly attended the press conference for the reopening.

Round the corner, I see the Uptown
Theatre, boarded up. Manager Tom
Malloy, now gone from his
house on Spruce Street where
he handed me lemons off the tree
last winter. I once climbed
the Uptown's carpeted stairways
to sit transfixed in the dark,
never imagining back then
that it would be over soon.

Napa High School, 1950s. *Courtesy of Napa County Historical Society.*

BASEBALL, BY THE NAPA HIGH SWIMMING POOL AND AT THE FAIRGROUNDS

Hoffman Avenue: 1952
Summers were hotter then, the fairgrounds dusty all day from drill team competition and real rodeos, back when locals united in the spirit of the wild west, comfortable inside the world of cattle and horses and the hoosegow. We grazed in the pasture aura of a county where the sheriff rode a horse and the August air smelled of prunes and hay and home-grown tomatoes.

Those summers in the Fifties we sat on cool cement porches, played Monopoly and Parcheesi, traded baseball cards that came in bags of Mother's Cookies, bartering and bickering in the shadow of the cemetery. We made gum from the melting asphalt on Hoffman Avenue, barbecued in back yards to the comfortable drone of the San Francisco Seals games broadcast over KFRC radio, our man announcing Elmer Singleton next at bat….
—Paula Amen Judah

Ellwin Jobe remembers playing Fly League baseball, "right in front of the Napa HS swimming pool which no longer exists since portable classrooms have now taken over that space"—as it looked onto Jefferson Street.

There was an A and a B division for each named team. The teams were represented by names such as Scorpions, Ants, Locusts, Beetles, Yellowjackets, Locusts, Spiders, Wasps and Termites. The ball was one sized closer to a baseball but a little larger and smaller than a softball, supposedly for player safety.

Marlene Wilson Hurley recalls: "The men who worked at Basalt would play a lot at Napa fairgrounds. It was an awesome full sized park with wood bleachers shaped behind home plate. There was a shake and drinks place too. The rivalry of course was a big deal. Stan Miller was a really good pitcher and hitter. We used to go and watch him play sometimes."

Fly League was disbanded in 1984 and was replaced by Little League.

MINI GOLF, DOWNTOWN NAPA

Once, families could play miniature golf—and rent paddleboats—on Third Street just east of Soscol. Kathleen Dreessen quotes from its final owner, Roger Bubel:

> *"We have a huge following. I sell hundreds of season passes and not just to kids, lots of adults play three, four times a week, some come from as far as San Francisco." At an admission price for children at $2, and a season pass at $10, it's a bargain that a family can enjoy. He doesn't even charge extra for children's birthday parties. This will be the last summer for Paradise Miniature Golf. "The flood control project needs the land," explained Bubel, who added that it's not a money-making venture and he won't relocate it.*

The min-golf course is gone for good, and a restaurant remains on the site.

DRIVE-IN ON FOSTER ROAD

The first drive-in movie theater in America opened in Camden, New Jersey, in 1933, the brainchild of a young man named Richard Hollingshead Jr., a manager at his father's auto shop. He dreamed of creating something that would bring a little fun to the tough daily life of the Depression era. By the 1950s, there were thousands of drive-ins across America. Children of that era remember parents reclining their seats, a father messing around with the weird little box on a pole next to the car window and the speaker crackling to life.

Napa got its own drive-in, the Kay-Von, by 1951. Rhonda Torres recalls: "Used to wait in line along Foster Road. Used to stop at Manny's on Imola Avenue to stock up on "goodies" prior to going to the show. Saw *Bonnie and Clyde* and *American Graffiti* when they first came out." Jim Ford remembers: "A typical mobile date in Napa in those days of yore might have been something like this: After picking up his date, the guy would drive to the Kay-Von Drive-In theater to watch a movie. After entering and parking at the theater and hanging a speaker on the inside of the driver window, the guy and the gal could sit back and watch the world news, a cartoon and perhaps a double feature, all from the comfort of the automobile."

Pat Stanley recalls, "I recall the sad day it was gutted by fire in the '70s. The sky was orange from the glow of the huge fire. An off-duty, rookie firefighter responded directly to the scene, but without his helmet and other firefighting gear. He asked me to drive him back to Station Two on Park Avenue to grab those essentials, then back to the fire. I felt like I was driving a fire chief's car without a red light or siren as I wheeled my little VW bug on my mission. It was fun."

The theater shut down in 1981. On the site now stands a condo complex.

BEL AIRE BOWL

Friends of all ages bowled at Napa Bowl and Bel Aire Bowl. Doug Murray recalls: "My mom was an avid bowler and participated in a league for as long as I can remember. Had her own bowling ball, shoes, etc. I joined a Sat morn league and stuck with it for several years, along with my buddy Wally Keller. Bowling was something we could do as a foursome on a double date."

Marlene Wilson Hurley adds, "And over at Bel Aire Bowl (the real IT place to be) the Clydesdale horses came and you could ride in the wagon." Terry Murphy Longoria adds:

> *Bel Aire Bowl was a great place to go and kind of grew with us. When Marc and I were dating, we joined leagues so we could play with friends and coworkers. The biggest issues were drinking—there was a full bar there and as the evening moved along it could get a little weird and smoking. Since there were no smoking rooms then—the bowlers smoked away. It was hard to breathe by the end of the night and when we went home the clothes*

Above: Kaiser Steel bowling team, 1960s. *Courtesy of Napa County Historical Society.*

Left: *From left to right*, Deanna and Dan Krueckemeier Fogerty, "Colonel Sanders" and Larry and Marion Dickerson at Bel Aire Bowl, 1969. *Courtesy of Deanna Krueckemeier Fogerty.*

> *went right in the washer. The cool thing though was that we made lots of friends—it was not dependent on the weather and we were able to have good fun and a little competition. I have more bowling trophies than from any other sport! They had arcade games there and they were among the first to have the computerized games like space invaders. We'd go over after work sometimes and just hang around to beat the score.*

Bel Aire Bowl opened in 1962 as the northernmost anchor to the Bel Aire shopping center, with twenty-four lanes, a restaurant and a full-service lounge. Michael Deyerle writes:

The twenty-four lanes were indeed state-of-the-art, with automatic pinsetters, overhead projection scoring and underground ball returns making for a sleek, albeit compact, fun center for then-modern Napa families. Later in the evening, the lounge would become stage to one of many fine live music bands blasting out current pop tunes to keep the locals dancing and enjoying the party into the wee hours.

Bel Aire filled all of its lanes in the prime 6:00 p.m. slot and again at 9:00 p.m., five days a week. Michael Deyerle recalls: "I met Napans from all walks of life during my many hours in these centers, from janitors and car salesmen to doctors and lawyers. Day care was provided at no charge to allow parents the night out without having to worry about leaving the little ones behind. You could literally check on your babies between frames."

Local businesses sponsored teams young and old alike, paying for bowling shirts with names emblazoned across team members' backs. Owner Jim Alonzi shared the love of his business with customers; bowlers and employees felt they were part of a much larger family.

Deanna Krueckemeier Fogerty remembers: "I loved Bel Aire Bowl. I was on the Tuesday morning housewives league and my husband at that time, Dan, and I were on a couples league on Friday evenings. We also would bowl for Blue Chip Stamps."

VICHY SPRINGS

Napa children treasured Vichy Springs, owned by Merle and Grace Harris between 1946 and 1967, which had a swimming pool open to the public. Vichy Springs and most of the surrounding lands had once been part of the Mexican land grant Rancho Yajome. Most of this watershed was wilderness area to at least 1869, and thereafter this portion of the Milliken Creek watershed was developed for pasture and grazing agricultural uses.

Jane Smith recalls: "It was nothing to walk from Second Street out to the end of Third Street, down the Silverado Trail to Monticello Road, to Vichy's, the only swimming tank in Napa, to swim all day and walk home again, pink and raw from sunburn." Some days, they had to wait while the tank was filled. Smith describes a Mrs. Briles, who "dispensed candy bars, drinks, gum, and rented rubber bathing caps summer after summer after summer. She was a judge, jury, mother, father, policeman, swimming teacher and lifeguard. A swim was ten cents." Doug Murray recalls: "I would ride my bicycle to the pool each morning after breakfast and chores. A later start to the day's fun made for much warmer swims and we would hang out there from morning until dusk. When we were not swimming we would play the pinball machines in the arcade alongside the pool entrance."

The Vichy site is covered over by country club homes. Cathy Mathews: "All that's left is what we remember. Hard to imagine that we had three swimming pools in this town."

For every Napan who misses the 1950s and '60s, there are new Napans who experienced play differently. Dr. Phong Vu, who picked pears as a child in the old asylum orchards at Napa College, came of age in the 1980s and '90s in Napa. His memories include: "Fishing with homemade fishing rods in the Napa River, smashing quarters on the Wine Train tracks, circus acts at the Napa Fairgrounds, duck feeding near Kennedy park, July Fourth fireworks on the Napa College soccer field, and even waking up to see people swimming in the streets during the 1986 flood."

Our two bowling alleys are now reduced to one, always packed on the weekends. Our skating rink and drive-in movie are gone, as are the rowdy bars where bands played and couples danced into the night. Pools are private or located at gyms or high schools. As Napans have lost places to play, Napa itself has been discovered as a place to play for out-of-towners.

5

WHERE WE SHOPPED

A flood changes things; the river with its possibilities for good and harm remain constant.

—Carol Kammen, *On Doing Local History*

TURN-OF-THE-CENTURY MAIN STREET

Some of the earliest Napa businesses were opened by Jewish immigrants. Freedman Levinson opened a general store on Main Street; Julius Salomonson originally sold dry goods and clothing and later entered the lumber business. In 1870, Herman Schwartz opened his hardware store in Napa. According to journalist Louis Ezettie, Schwartz told his customers, "Doing my own work (roofing, tinning, and plumbing), I can do it cheaper than anyone can." Schwartz sold stoves, glass and fruit cans "at San Francisco prices," as well as agricultural equipment, making his store a gathering place for farmers and fishermen. Brother Max Schwartz opened a cigar and liquor store nearby on Main Street.

Another brother, Joseph, opened a shop called the City of Paris and built a Victorian-style house on the northeast corner of Oak and Franklin, one of the few with indoor plumbing in 1890. He and his wife, Adelhide, were the proud parents of Irving Schwartz and the grandparents of Harvey Schwartz, a historian in the Bay Area. The whole block near the Opera House was sometimes called the "Schwartz Block."

Right: Joseph Schwartz with his wife, Adelheid Vogel Schwartz. *Courtesy of Harvey Schwartz.*

Below: Abe Strauss clothing store, Napa. *Courtesy of Napa County Historical Society.*

Bryant's Candy, Napa. *Courtesy of Napa County Historical Society.*

Charlie Levinson, son of Freedman, joined forces with Abe Strauss and opened a clothing store specializing in menswear. Charlie's brother Joe became a pharmacist and operated Levinson's Pharmacy on Main and First for many decades, frequently bartering his goods for services and earning the nickname "Pills."

Napa's favorite sweet shop, Bryant's Candy Store and Fountain, opened at 1134 First Street on June 14, 1928. It was owned and operated by Edward and Emma Bryant. Rebecca Yerger writes: "The store's interior was beautifully appointed with fine woods, marble and harlequin flooring. Just sitting at the fountain bar was probably a treat with its mahogany woodwork, pink Tennessee marble top trimmed with Verdi marble. The booths and table sets were also crafted from mahogany."

ITALIAN GROCERIES, "LITTLE ITALY"

Napa was populated by Italian immigrants in the first part of the twentieth century, some of whom opened grocery stores. Augustine Giovannoni arrived in San Francisco from Italy and moved to Napa in the early 1920s.

He worked in a quicksilver mine in Calistoga. Augustine married Josephine Lanaro, and they opened Giovannoni's Market, across from Churchill Manor. The family lived on the second floor and ran the market on the first floor. Augustine worked as a painter at a local shipyard and drove a horse-drawn ice cream cart.

Son Larry Giovannoni recalled his boyhood: "I remember going around with my father to get grocery orders. Most people didn't have a phone." After going door-to-door taking orders, they would return later with the deliveries. Augustine Giovannoni picked up groceries at the wharf down the block from the corner of Oak and Brown. After unloading cargo, the boats packed fruit from Napa orchards to carry back to San Francisco.

Giuseppe Vallergas operated a truck garden on the Napa River in the 1880s, providing the town with fresh vegetables. In 1947, son Joe opened Vallergas Drive-In Market on the corner of First and Juarez. In 1955, he built a second market behind the first one and hauled the first store across the river. The store was so popular that he opened a Redwood Road store in 1962 and a River Park store in 1964. The Giovannonis sold their market

Former site of beloved Vallerga's Market, Redwood Road. *Courtesy of Adaira Grohs.*

to Ignacio Magallanes in 2007, but they still operate Browns Valley Market. The three Vallergas stores closed one by one in the early twenty-first century, until the last one closed in 2019, mourned by thousands of grateful customers.

Saying goodbye
to the aisles where you
know every can's space.
Goodbye to Joey at the register
who remembers loading
your truck—ten years ago,
when he was a bagger.
He's lost his job because
building another hotel
brings profit for someone.
The cost of change: a small store
built by Italian immigrants,
here a half century, gone.

Downtown Napa in the 1950s

Ray Guadagni grew up in Italian Napa. He has vivid memories of shopping downtown in the 1950s and '60s: "Napa Music Store usually had young guys and gals hanging out, trying out records. Upstairs, you could get a record and bring it into a booth to play it, listen to it and see if you wanted to purchase it....A block over on Coombs Street was Adamo Music Center—another cool music store with all the latest releases, as well as sheet music. My big trick here was to study the sheet music of a song I wanted to learn. If it was a simple song I could memorize it, run home, play it on my accordion and commit it to memory."

Nick Cervone began working at a tailor's shop in Italy at the age of six. In 1949, he immigrated to the United States with his father. When he saw the Golden Gate Bridge, it reminded him of the harbor at Naples, and the Napa vineyards reminded him of Italy. The Cervones opened their tailor shop on Second Street in Napa in 1955, sewing while opera music soared out of the radio. Ray Guadagni remembers, "Mr. Cervone plays the mandolin, and when I was a little boy, my parents would take me to his house where Nick would play his mandolin and I would play my accordion."

Above: Postcard of downtown Napa, late 1950s. *Courtesy of Mr. M.*

Right: Tailor Nick Cervone. *Courtesy of Lauren Coodley*.

Carithers was the major tenant in the old Behlow Building, a stone edifice that had withstood the 1906 San Francisco earthquake with little damage. It was located at the corner of Second and Brown Streets, across from Napa's historic courthouse. Carithers Department Store sold clothes for men, women and children. Ray Guadagni describes its pneumatic tube system: "The sales lady would put the money Mom gave her for the purchase of an item into a cylindrical container, and it would then travel through a network of tubes by compressed air or by vacuum to the cashier sitting upstairs in an office. The cashier would then complete the transaction and put Mom's change along with a receipt in the cylindrical container for the return trip to the sales lady."

Jim Ford recalled his own experience with Carithers, being hired as a thirteen-year-old: "I was hired as the janitor and shipping and receiving clerk. The job paid fifty cents an hour, I got a 10 percent employee discount on any merchandise I might purchase and they worked around my split-shift junior high school hours."

Levi's jeans were among the attractions of the store. Because of the war effort, the maker of Levi's had to devote most of its production to items for the military. As a result, the making of jeans was secondary, and they were hard to come by. Ford recalls: "Since I was the shipping and receiving clerk, I knew when Levi's arrived—and they only came in a few pairs at a time....I was usually the first one in line for them. My classmates at school were very envious. (Levi's were then $2.25 a pair.)"

BREWSTERS

In 1960, when her husband, Larry, and her brother Harris Nussbaum became partners with her father running Brewsters, Rachel Friedman arrived with Larry and two young children. Back then, Napa had a population of about fifteen thousand people. Rachel remembers: "When I first moved to Napa, my comment was 'I feel like I'm moving to the end of the world.'" Trancas was the north edge of town, uncrowded and barely developed with only the newly built hospital and some Italian and Chinese restaurants, reflective of Napa's early immigrants. The Friedmans bought a home in the just-built Bel Aire subdivision. Rachel remembers that "Bel Aire Plaza housed only Montgomery Ward, the bowling alley, and Levinson's Drugs, which had moved out there." But, Rachel remembers, it was "no competition for shopping—everyone went downtown."

Early Brewsters, Napa. *Courtesy of Rachel Friedman.*

She describes Napa in those days as a "real country town where everyone was very friendly." Brewsters supplied work clothes, boots, bedding, cots and almost anything else the vineyard workers needed to survive; when the store had an outdoor sale, shoppers lined up for blocks. Louis Martini would drive up in his Cadillac clad in overalls. The Brewsters ads were a highlight of the *Napa Register*, with their zany caricatures of Rachel, Larry and the crew.

Ray Guadagni remembers: "One of my greatest pleasures as a youngster came on Sundays after Mass, on the walk back home, when I stopped at Brewster's. There, I could talk to a sweet man who worked there named Harry Greco, the brother of Napa's mayor, Joe Greco. I could browse through all the World War II surplus equipment, including gas masks, machetes, knives, bayonets, Army coats, Navy pea jackets, and so much more."

In the seventies, while some Napans favored what looked like a revitalization of downtown, many businesspeople questioned the benefits of redevelopment. A group of Main Street merchants formed "Citizens against the Destruction of Napa," using Brewsters as a meeting place. Friedman's husband, Larry, particularly opposed the construction of a clock tower on First Street and took his fight all the way to the California Supreme Court, where the case was lost. Kevin Courtney recalls: "When the city leveled the heart of downtown for new stores in the 1970s, it celebrated by erecting a

Left: A young Rachel Friedman with her children, 1960s. *Right*: Rachel and Larry Friedman, owners of Brewsters. *Courtesy of Rachel Friedman.*

clock tower. Standing 72 feet high with four illuminated faces, exploding crossbeams tipped with light globes and chimes that played snappy tunes, the tower was meant to symbolize downtown's rebirth. Instead, it came to symbolize the public's skepticism with urban renewal."

Architect Hideo Sasaki came to Napa for the clock tower's dedication in July 1974 and reflected on his creation. "As time goes by, the peal of Napa's chimes will earn a nostalgic niche in the minds of its inhabitants."

GROCERY STORES, DOWNTOWN NAPA

Wash Mannering was a member of the Garment Workers Union and had been secretary and president of the Napa Labor Council. He left his job as a fabric worker at Cameron Shirt to open Mannering's Grocery Store, which he operated with his wife, Marian, at the corner of Oak and Seymour for fifty years. Rena Johnson describes how Marian Mannering ran the grocery store at Seymour and Oak Streets, "It was a two-story house, and they lived on the top floor. Wash worked cutting shirts at Cameron Shirt Company, great big stacks of them, while his wife ran the store. She helped lots of people during the Depression, letting them pay on credit—how they did it, I don't know." Ken Munk, nephew of Wash Mannering, recalls: "The

Top: Closing of Allen and Benedicts. *Courtesy of Jeff Doran.*

Bottom: Line of people waiting to go in Allen and Benedicts, 1994. *Courtesy of Jeff Doran.*

old-timers who may have worked at Cameron Shirt Factory came to 'the store' for homemade sandwiches made by Aunt Marian and her sisters in the kitchen behind the store.…I was the stock boy stocking shelves. I always liked to hear Uncle Wash call to me from behind the butcher counter with a hearty, 'Hey K Munk,' whenever I would show up."

Safeway was at Jefferson and Clay Streets. Patty Langer recalls walking there with her mother, with Darr's five-and-dime store next door. Sometimes, they stopped at the counter at Woolworth's to order hot fudge sundaes or banana splits. The area now home to the Factory Outlets once held Purity Market, Allen and Benedict and the Saddle Shop, and she and her family could walk across the road to shop. There was no freeway: Highway 29 was just a stop sign. Allen and Benedict and other stores closed in 1994, to be replaced by Factory Outlets.

UPVALLEY STORES

Yountville's Cash 'n' Carry was owned and operated by Bud and Barbara Dulinsky. Years later, the building was enlarged and remodeled. Today, Yountville residents know the site as Ranch Market Two.

In St. Helena, Greta Ericson opened a dress shop in 1968 in an old stone building. The building was erected in 1890 on the corner of Hunt and Main Streets. She named her store Wine Country Clothes. Ericson recalls: "I named that building Cornerstone, because after I sold the dress shop [in 1980] I ran a hotel that was above the dress shop and refurbished the top of that building. Before that, it was called the Valley Hotel...for people living on Social Security; the room was rented for ten dollars a night."

The building is now Reeds, a high-end women's clothing store. Jesse Duarte adds to Greta's story: "What she considered her greatest accomplishment

Yountville's Cash 'n' Carry, as it appeared in 1963. *Courtesy of Barbara and Bud Dulinsky.*

was still to come. She recalled her friendship with Jean Rianda, who owned the house that's now the senior center. 'Jean initially wanted to leave her house to me, but I suggested that she leave it to become a senior center.... Jean stipulated this in her will that I, Greta, would make it happen.'"

In St. Helena, Goodman's Department Store was also a big attraction from the 1940s through the 1980s. Cathy Mathews remembers: "You could get work clothes through going to town clothes. It was two stories, across the street from what is now the Cameo Theatre."

FULL SERVICE GAS STATIONS, NAPA AND YOUNTVILLE

And there's where (during the day) mom would stop for gas,
a Shell filling station in the curve at the foot of a long hill,
a couple of pumps and a little office and a double bay
over which "Service Is Our Business" shone in red plastic
—Michael McFee, "Service Is Our Business"

After World War II, affordable cars and access to cheap gasoline created an economy in which most families were able to buy a car. In Yountville, Flock's Garage was the main gas station. It was located just north of the Saint Joan of Arc Catholic Church on Highway 29. Millard Flock opened the repair shop in 1929. In the late 1940s, he expanded it, doubling in size. Vernon Flock, Millard's grandson, remembered his early years working at his grandpa's service station. There was a large pit in the ground where cars got oil changes. In the days before hydraulic lifts, attendants would drive the cars over a pit and go down a ladder to drain the oil.

Cathy Mathews describes John Grippi's Flying A station on Silverado Trail: "My grandmother loved him....John would look under the hood and say, 'Mrs. Russell, there's a little something wrong. You need to take it to Vito Grossi's [next to the fairgrounds].' You got your windshield done every time, and he always checked your wipers and your oil."

Mathews also remembers Primo Colla's Shell station on Lincoln and Silverado: "An incredibly good-looking guy, one of the first people in town to have a car wash." In 2007, *Register* writer Pat Stanley noted the change of ownership of Colla's Shell at Lincoln Avenue and Silverado Trail. It was sold by proprietor Larry Hansen after twenty-eight years. Stanley writes:

Flock's Garage, Yountville, mid-1940s. *Courtesy of Vernon Flock.*

Millard Flock (*right*) and service station attendant Paul Chastain in their uniforms, 1940s. *Courtesy of Vernon Flock.*

> *Hansen has been a familiar figure in front of the station, waving to friends and customers, smoking a pipe or walking his 7-year-old Jack Russell terrier, Billie, when not pumping gas. This year, 45 days of rain within two months kept customers away from the car wash he installed 18 years ago: "Not many people pay for a car wash when God will wash it for free," he said.*

Gas was fifty-seven cents a gallon when Hansen opened the doors in February 1978, purchasing it from the handsome Primo Colla. Patrick Scott was hired while still in high school and eventually became station manager; at one time or another, Scott's four brothers also worked at Colla's Shell. As many as five different families have been supported by the station. Pat Stanley notes: "Hansen, sixty, said he's too young to retire. 'I cannot not work,' he said. 'I'll get a job. I can't stop working.' 'I'll really miss seeing my friends and customers,' he said. 'That's what I enjoyed the most. I'll dearly miss them and want to thank Napa.'"

Lincoln and Silverado was one of the last full-service gas stations in town, until about 2000. The Flying A gas station remains on Silverado Trail but has been closed for decades.

Milt Totman helps Nils McCune clean the windshield at his service station, 1988. *Courtesy of Lauren Coodley.*

THE CLOSING OF CARITHERS

In Napa, clerks at Carithers, the last union department store in Napa, went on strike when they were asked to take a pay cut in 1981. The Women's Political Caucus collected canned food for the strikers and organized benefits, including movie nights and dances at the Labor Temple on Main Street. Inspired by films documenting women's early labor struggles, the youngest striker, nineteen, brought her infant to the picket line in a stroller adorned with a sign reading "Don't Be a Scab."

Linda Dietiker-Yolo, member of the Napa County Commission on the Status of Women, wrote to the manager of Carithers: "If the shocking plight of these women is not entirely as represented, perhaps you will inform us. Otherwise, we ask that justice be instituted at Carithers." The women won their strike, and they credited the community for its support. Carithers striker Bonnie Lee Barnhill described their victory as "one giant step for womankind." From their newsletter: "It was like David slaying Goliath: a relative handful of determined union women picketed their employer, Carithers, part of a mammoth corporation—in order to maintain a decent living standard and win dignity in their place of work. They never gave up.

Clerks at Carithers on strike, 1981. *Courtesy of Lauren Coodley.*

Carithers clerks in front of the store, 1981. *Courtesy of Lauren Coodley.*

They walked for four and one half months, from the beginning of spring on through the parching heat of summer."

Yet, one by one, the unionized clothing corporations in America shut down. Clothes for Americans were made in sweatshops around the world. As clothes became cheaper and cheaper, wages and conditions in retail stores plummeted in Napa and throughout the nation. Carithers closed its doors in 1985.

BATTLE OVER BIG-BOX STORES, SOSCOL

In 1986, the most devastating flood in one hundred years hit the town, as the Napa River rose to levels no one living had seen before. Nearly five thousand people were evacuated, 250 homes were destroyed and three people died. Soscol Avenue turned into a river, most of Napa's businesses were damaged from the floodwaters and the downtown stores were drenched with mud. According to the *Register*: "Larry Friedman thanked his employees for saving the rest of the store by stacking sandbags until almost midnight; nobody has flood insurance. 'If there's such a thing as an off the floor sale we'll have one,' Friedman joked."

But the drought years that followed eliminated Brewsters' wet gear business. Two years after the flood, the town council voted to approve a Target Store in the Bel Aire shopping center, and Brewsters lost much of its camping gear sales. In 1998, when no buyer for the store could be found, Larry and Rachel decided it was time to close. Kevin Courtney reported: "News of Brewster's demise had shaken a lot of old-time customers. I had a woman break into tears. She said, 'What am I going to do? I've been coming here as a child.' When Larry made an appearance at the store Tuesday, a shopper came up to the busy shopkeeper and whispered, 'This is history.'"

Around the corner from the clock tower, throughout the 1970s, '80s and '90s, Sandi Perlman owned Tees and Tops, which supplied customized sports uniforms to local teams. When her landlord tripled her rent, hoping to bring in upscale retailers, she concluded that she would have to close her store. "It's a fist in the gut," Perlman told Kevin Courtney. "I sell $25 items. I can't get away from that. That's who I am."

Like small towns across the country, Napa residents fought and ultimately lost the battle to keep discount chain stores out. In 1996, several "big box" stores were built on wetlands in south Napa, creating an enormous

Clock tower, downtown Napa, late 1990s. *Courtesy of Lauren Coodley.*

shopping development that threatened the existence of local businesses and department stores. Within a few years, Napa lost Woolworth's, J.C. Penney's, Montgomery Ward and Merrill's Drugstore, sources of both jobs and cherished memories for townspeople.

Bruce Baird reported that when Woolworth's closed, tears ran down the face of seventy-two-year-old Myrtle Alric "as dozens of locals expressed their thanks to Alric and the rest of the staff at the lunch counter." Baird added that "black balloons and ribbons marking the death of the downtown institution hung on the booths." Even the managers of the Downtown Promotional District and the Napa Valley Conference Bureau dressed in black, while regulars at the luncheonette "pinned the waitresses with black carnations between orders of fries and refills of coffee." Brenda Gee brought her son in honor of her own parents bringing her to the counter twenty years before: "It's just like I remember it—the lights are old and the smells are the same."

Kevin Courtney described the fate of the clock tower in 2000:

> *The tower had fallen on hard times. The chimes didn't work. All four clock faces were broken. It had become the butt of jokes. Getting everything back into working order would have cost $50,000 or more. Or for half that, the city could tear it down. It wasn't even a close call. The City Council unanimously voted to end the clock tower debate and raze it.*

Unlike Napa, Calistoga and St. Helena have maintained many of their original small businesses and successfully resisted big-box stores.

LOST IN THE TWENTY-FIRST CENTURY: NORMAR, FAMILY DRUG AND GOLDEN CARROT

Norma Arndt decided to open her fabric store so she would have a source of money for college scholarships to 4-H students. Arndt's husband found the building at 1327 Main Street. When she moved to Napa in 1955, the population was five thousand.

She told Alisha Wyman:

> *"It's hard work, though, and sometimes it can be dirty, dusty, but I loved every bit of it." To this day, she does all of the fabric buying and pricing for the store during the four afternoons each week she comes in. The store is filled with thick bolts of fabrics, from cottons to laces to patterns. One shelf*

is filled with boxes of buttons, each marked by a button sewn to the outside of the boxes. Thread in every shade of the rainbow is on display on one rack.... Arndt still makes all of her own clothing. On a recent afternoon, she wore a green pair of velveteen pants she had made, as well as a maroon, green and orange jacket and scarf.

Normar closed its doors in 2014. Sudie Pollock writes: "The place I miss the most is Normar." Her students learned to sew at Hill and Valley Teen Parent Program: "Norma Arndt had the most gorgeous fabrics upstairs—I made a prom dress for a girl from fabric she picked out. It was such fun to make her dream come true. For years, I purchased fabric for my pregnant students at Normar, to make flannel-backed baby quilts."

Family Drug was opened by Mary Doud. Born in San Francisco, Mary grew up in the Outer Mission. Both of her parents were immigrants from northern Italy. Her aunt and uncle owned a grocery store where her parents met. She would play with an old scale, filling bottles and pillboxes and weighing them. Her family had always visited the Napa Valley, where her dad would graft grape vines while she and her mother stayed at Stags Leap. They would take the ferry to Vallejo and then the electric railway to Yountville, where a car from the resort would pick them up.

At thirteen, she began translating for a dentist's Italian patients, continuing through high school and business college. She took the streetcar to the UCSF College of Pharmacy on Parnassus "and marched in with my credentials and said I want to go to college. I want to be a pharmacist." Mary was the youngest in her class and one of only six women.

By age twenty-one, she had worked in many pharmacies in San Francisco and soon married her first husband, Richard Pescaro. In 1951, they heard that Arighi and Ballerina Pharmacy at 949 Brown Street was for sale. Mary and Richard bought the business, moved from San Francisco and rented "a lovely stone house" at Stags Leap after the resort closed. In the early fifties, "Mary heard about a new shopping area now known as Food City. She negotiated with the landlord, Sam Gordon, and got three months free rent. The fixtures were installed on a one-year credit basis. Later, she consolidated to just that one store on Old Sonoma Road, which she enlarged several times. Mr. Gordon, who always called her Sis, helped with remodeling costs. She and Richard continued to operate both stores until his death in 1954."

Mary became the first secretary of the Napa County Pharmacy Association in 1956, then the president of Napa Solano Pharmacy Association in 1965. She founded two scholarships for a high school and a junior college student

Former site of Normar Fabric Store, Main Street, Napa. *Courtesy of Adaira Grohs.*

Sam Gordon developed Food City in the late 1930s, one of the very few Art Moderne buildings in Napa County. *Courtesy of the Napa County Historical Society.*

and was named Pharmacist of the Month by the Northern California Pharmacy Association. Her scrapbook includes many cards thanking her for her talk about the history of perfume. Family Drug featured over two hundred different scents, while the selection of jewelry was one of Mary's specialties, along with her interest in encouraging young people.

Tom Gracia came to work for Mary as a pharmacist in 1976 and became a partner. Tom Gracia's wife, Roxann, remembers:

> *I said I would come to California, if there was a nice place for my horses and clean air! Tom talked to Mary, and we moved to Napa in 1976. In the early years, Tom and I started helping to market the front end of the store, something Mary had not done. I remember coming in after work as a pharmacist at Vallejo General, now Sutter Solano, and having the kids sit and crawl around as we rearranged shelves and unpacked sale items.*

Tom died in 2016. Roxann remembers Tom's effect on the community:

> *He always had a smile and would never let anything of the day upset him. He was the Hospice pharmacist for years. He'd get called in the middle of the night or during a holiday dinner and never got paid for the extra trips in to fill a prescription. "Someone needed his help." Tom wrote off a lot of accounts to the under-privileged. We never received help or donations, but managed to give whatever was needed. We were very proud of the fact that we remained open during the worst recession of our time. Our employees had jobs. We filled the needs for people and animals…at one time we provided meds for exotic animals at Marine World and unique items for all kinds of pets.*

Family Drug closed in November 2019. Tom's son Joseph continues the family tradition at the newly opened Family Medical at 592 Lincoln Avenue. He and his wife, Neanna, are certified fitters for garments and other equipment.

When Lorna Birdsall, owner-operator of the Golden Carrot natural foods store in River Park Center for the past twenty-nine years, closed her store in 2014, she told a reporter, "I'm grateful to the community for the support they've given and the faith they've had in me for 29 years. A lot of people these days don't have community, and I've had the most wonderful community."

After the earthquake in 2000 smashed up most of the store, she came to work the next morning and found nine customers waiting to help sweep up rubble and hose off the floor. "I served a generation of families, and then

Lorna Birdsall and her daughter Hailey. *Courtesy of Lorna Birdsall.*

the children of those families. And some of my employees have been the children of former employees."

A small square of a shop, back
when shops were small and owned
by people. You could grind peanuts
into butter in the corner, sometimes
find vegan tuna sandwiches, always
vitamins, breads, noodles, fruit.

Like our lives, we thought it would
be golden forever. That Lorna would
always come out of the back ready to
share her healing wisecraft. So many
ailments were cured by her advice,

But the one that stays with me is
golden, like her store, like her glow.
Buy goldenseal to save your gums,
she told me, and I keep it still, in
my room, in its corner. It offers
Me a reminder every night, of when once
there was a little square corner store
And a wise woman to run it.

6

LOST NATURE

Before there were trucks and stereo systems, tract houses and motorcycles, the air was filled with other sounds. It was the roar of nature that set the evening ambience: a hubbub generated by millions of water fowl, amphibians, beetles, bugs, and birds, grasshoppers and a myriad of other creatures that thrived in the small lakes and ponds and wetlands.

—Joseph Amato, *Rethinking Home*

A thousand years ago, Napa was home to an abundance of wildlife. Napa settlers' early records include mention of the California condor. With a wingspan of nearly ten feet, condors could soar on thermal updrafts for hours and reach fifteen hundred feet. The California Clapper Rail, now listed as endangered and often impossible to find, was once so numerous that residents ate it.

For millennia, the valley floor was covered with oak woodland, providing homes for deer, antelope, tule elk, black bear and grizzly bear, mountain lion and quail. The Napa River held freshwater eel, trout, steelhead salmon, ducks and otters, and the skies were thick with birds.

The valley floor was also home to vernal pools, small seasonal wetlands formed when winter rains fill a depression in impermeable ground. The vernal pools allowed fairy shrimp and other freshwater crustaceans to hatch, salamanders and spadefoot toads to mate and migrant waterfowl to feed. Waterfowl like the cinnamon teal and ruddy duck nested in the valley's freshwater marshes but are now largely limited to marginal sites at reservoirs

Valley Quail. *Courtesy of McGill Library, UnSplash.*

Beaver. *Courtesy of Niklas Hamann, UnSplash.*

and wastewater treatment plants. The now-rare tricolored blackbird likely nested in the cattails and rules of the valley's marshes, while red-legged frogs probably bred in the open water. Changes to the riparian habitat along the Napa River and to the wetlands that once stretched all the way to Imola Avenue also reduced the prevalence of many bird species in the county.

Nineteenth-century trappers hunted otters, seals, beavers and minks to near extinction by the 1840s. But before that time, beaver dams increased the extent and persistence of wetlands and ponds along the river even beyond the amount documented in the 1850s and '60s, providing a range of ecosystem functions. By building dams from riparian trees, beavers create areas of temporary flooding that capture fine sediment, prevent channel incision and enhance summer base flow.

BIRDWATCHING, NAPA

Banker and Boy Scout leader Elmer Bickford wrote a letter to the *Register* in 1925, listing the birds that the Scouts had sighted on one weekend. Bickford was one of the leading citizens of nineteenth-century Napa and an outstanding amateur photographer. He bought one of the town's first cars in 1904. He became the president of the First National Bank on First Street and co-founded the Boy Scouts of Napa. Along with his Scouts, he listed the birds he found. Justine Fournier compared this list with *Breeding Birds of Napa*, published by the Solano/Napa Audubon Society. The birds that had disappeared by 2008 included the following:

> *Green-backed Goldfinch, English Sparrow, Ruby-crowned Kinglet, Plain Titmouse, Audubon Warbler, Valley Quail, Red-shafted Flicker, White-crowned Sparrow, Red-breasted Sapsucker, Townsend Solitaire, Rufous Hummingbird, Lute-scent Warbler, Golden-crowned Sparrow, Rough-winged Swallow, Slender-build Nuthatch, Willow Goldfinch, Nicasio (Bewick) Wren, Western, Western Flycatcher, Russet-backed Thrush, Cliff, Swallow, Wren Tit, Western Gnatcatcher, Long-tailed Chat, Pileolated Warbler, Pacific Yellow Throat, California Creeper, Arkansas Kingbird, Shrike, Mourning Dove, and Wood Duck, Horned Lark, Sparrow Hawk, Least Sandpiper, Western Sandpiper, Marbled Godwit, Hudsonian Curlew, Tule Wren, Bonaparte Gull, Herring Gull, Salt Marsh, Yellowthroat Coot, American Egret, Spoonbill Duck, Semipalmated Plover.*

Harvey Schwartz explains that his father, Irving, whose parents owned the City of Paris department store, was the second or third Eagle Scout in Napa. "When he was in the Scouts there were so many birds in Napa that it was possible to identify something like fifty different kinds....In later years, the scouts reduced the number of birds you had to identify to earn the Bird Watching merit badge."

Irving Schwartz, age three. *Courtesy of Harvey Schwartz.*

In 1945, *Audubon Magazine* named Cameron shirt cutter Carl Franco as part of a group that traveled to "Tulocay Cemetery, Henry Lane, Bush Creek from Waterworks to Little Trancas, along the road to Big Trancas and up Napa river 3/4 mile: upland pasture 50%, wooded creek bed 30%, lightly wooded upland 20%." It was December 31, and the eight people traveled ten miles, noting birds that included the Western Bluebird, the Golden Crowned Kinglet, Cedar Waxwing, Western Meadowlark and the California Purple Finch.

UPVALLEY PLANTS AND FLOWERS IN NAPA

Willis Jepson collected plants along the river at the Pope Street Bridge in St. Helena as early as 1892 and as late as 1936 on the way to botanizing Howell Mountain to the east. Among his findings: wetland species like water smartweed, nutsedge and basket sedge (which formed "stools 1 to 2 feet broad and 2 to 3 feet high in the flood bed"); more xeric plants like California brickell bush on "Flats"; five species of willow (red, arroyo, shining, Scouler's and narrowleaf); wild grape and a "fine cluster" of California (big-leaf) maple forty-five feet high. Further downstream, in 1934, Jepson notes: "Driving south in Napa Valley, one finds, a quarter of a mile north of Oakville...a wide open field stretching away to a screening border of splendid Valley Oak and tall Red Willow and Yellow Willow along the Napa River." Conservationist Tony Norris comments:

> *Around 95% of Quercus lobata, California white oak have been removed from Napa Valley. Most of these removals have occurred within living*

memory. It would be a fair estimate to suspect that better than 95% of the typical understory native bunch grass around those oaks, Nassella pulchra, purple needle grass has also been removed. Other species dependent on that oak/grass habitat relationship were certain to have been affected too. Invasive plants exacerbate the decline of native species. Ground nesting native bumble bees in the natural woodland meadow interfaces are declining as their range is narrowed and fragmented and selection of exotic plant species with pollen become far too specific and seasonal to sustain them year long. Wetland species are particularly hard hit by development and pollution.

Nineteenth-century accounts describe numerous fields of wildflowers in Napa. In 1853, Harley Harris Bartlett wrote that "wild flowers of varied hues were thickly scattered around" in the land that we now call American Canyon. Heading north from Oak Knoll, Bartlett noted "a luxuriant growth of grass, studded with brilliant wildflowers" and described the valley as "surrounded by a world of wildflowers of most gorgeous hues, which covered the plains on either side and loaded the air with rich perfume." Willis Jepson remembers "a radiant springtime when for four glorious weeks

Lupine. *Courtesy of Mercades Mehling, UnSplash.*

I botanized the whole length of the valley…cream cups, poppies, clover, filled the meadows and fields." Robin Grossinger notes that the loss of this remarkable expression of local climate and ecology is a largely overlooked transformation of the landscape: "Native wildflower seed banks lie intact waiting for the right conditions to return."

Cameron shirt cutter Carl Franco also collected specimens of ninety-six flowers. Flower pressing was one way to capture and preserve the beauty of the natural world. A plant press was two large flat boards surrounding alternating stacks of paper. Plants were kept tight with adjustable straps. On each page on which he preserved a specimen, he noted its Latin name, a common name and a location. He found flowers such as Blue Larkspur, Western Buttercup and Woodland Star on Soda Spring Road in April 1929. He preserved a Wild Iris from Dry Creek Road in June 1929. He found a Yellow Tulip on Redwood Road in May 1929. His last entry is a Lupine, location unspecified, in 1932.

Carolyn Parr Nature Center docent Karen Swain received Carl Franco's drawings from the Napa County Historical Society and preserved them into a scrapbook in 2007.

LITTLE TRANCAS BRIDGE, SARCO CREEK

The bridge was at the uppermost tidal line of the river and so provided a reliable source of fresh water uncontaminated by the brackish and salty water that moved up the river with the high tide. It was used as a regular crossing by horses and wagons, probably because it was the point farthest south in the valley not affected by tidal changes in the level of the river.

North from the Little Trancas Bridge was a natural slough off of the Napa River based on an 1837 survey of the old Yajome Spanish Land Grant. Like most of the sloughs in the valley, it was cut off from the river at some point in the ensuing century and the banks were clearly built up by levees. But the sloughs or side channels provided runoff relief from the main branch of the river during flood events. They also kept widespread wetlands thriving in the valley floor northward up the valley from Napa until many were filled in or cut off from the river. Doug Murray recalls:

> *In 1952, we moved to Woodside Drive just off of Monticello Road. Beyond the back fence of our yard my world opened onto a large fruit orchard bordered to the south by another large acreage of open fields*

Horses watering at Little Trancas Bridge. *Courtesy of the Napa County Historical Society.*

seasonally devoted to grazing sheep. It was the property of an old hermit and rancher, Louis Gasser, who would intermittently run me out of his orchard or in turn invite me to climb up on the two mule-drawn buckboard wagon he rode around his ranch for as long as I lived there. The southern border of Gasser's Ranch was marked by Sarco Creek. It was exploring those orchards, fields and creek beyond my backyard fence that became the defining feature of my Napa Valley childhood.

Some of the most exciting denizens of the summer creek bed were snakes. Garter snakes, with yellow stripes and sometimes red and blue side bands running the length of their bodies, would slide quickly into the underbrush or across a pool. Occasionally, I would spot the tan markings of bigger gopher snakes tucked in under the roots of a tree along the bank. But most spectacular of all were the black-and-white-banded king snakes. These were truly the most wondrous creatures. Some would reach lengths well over four feet. They were not aggressive, nor were they welcoming to a child's touch. They were best appreciated from a short distance. Sometimes, I would just squat on the ground a few feet away and watch a large king snake. It would stare back for a time, flicking its tongue at me, then glide effortlessly back into the undergrowth as if to say, nice visiting with you but I have more pressing matters to attend to than a gawking little freckle-faced kid.

Doug Murray with his fishing pole, Napa, around 1960. *Courtesy of Doug Murray.*

The open meadow of Murray's childhood is now a vineyard for the wine industry. Milliken Creek under the old stone bridge on Trancas is a homeless encampment, and the old Water Works at the East Side Reservoir are trophy homes. Murray concludes: "I would say the one mile radius of my childhood's natural world has captured the changes that have transformed the Napa Valley more broadly in the half-century-plus since my departure, wouldn't you?"

NAPA CREEK, WEST NAPA

Jeff Johnson writes of a similar experience to that of Doug Murray, over on the west side of town.

> *In 1955, my folks decided to move to a new neighborhood and found a beautiful country home just off West Lincoln Avenue, England Lane. My brother and I would begin attending the new West Park Elementary School. I met my best friends Mike Anderson, Bill Cox, Walter Trethaway and Steve Hicks.*
>
> *Together, we all played around the area including exploring Napa Creek at the end of West Pueblo Ave. and the walnut orchard directly next to our home on England Lane. In this orchard we would climb the trees, build mustard green forts, use our vivid imaginations to invent games and explore a wonderful barn and corral that contained cows and horses directly adjacent to my house. Still today, as I drive by on Highway 29, I look over occasionally to see the huge pine trees in our old backyard that Dad, my brother Greg and I planted as seedlings years ago.*
>
> *One of our favorite past times was playing in Napa Creek (when it dried up of course in the summer) at the end of West Pueblo Ave. Here was a treasure house of old tin cans, blackberry bush vines, lots of mud puddles to find polliwogs, and occasional snakes. Hidden in the various vines on the sides of the creek was an old car wreck worthy of constant exploring. One particular day, while playing in the creek, I found an old rock and subsequently its counterpart, a hollowed out stone that turned out to be an ancient Native American grinding rock and pestle. This artifact, which at the time meant little in the idea of preserving history, sat around and collected dust. When I became a teacher in Napa, I chose to include it as part of my teaching materials of California History.*

BATTLE OVER NAPA WETLANDS, IMOLA

There's been thousands of acres converted from wildland to grapes in the hills (mostly chaparral and grassland, some forest), and about a thousand acres converted from grapes to urban uses (mostly winery/tourism development and expansions) on the valley floor. Certainly, many once lovely natural spots are no longer so. There is a loss of social structure that pairs with commercial/industrial

development and skyrocketing land values. Rural communities are losing their tight-knit relations as elders die and children sell.
—Amber Manfree, geographer

In 1930, there were only 6,437 people living in Napa. In the 1940s, new houses were built on the streets called Ash, Sycamore and Spruce, where perhaps those trees once stood in open meadows. In the fifties and sixties, new houses were built north of Lincoln, in what had been farms; on the north side of Trancas, in an area named Bel Aire, and then in Browns Valley, were acres of prune orchards and dairy cows. By 1970, Napa had 37,000 people.

The population voted in a 1973 referendum to maintain the size of the city and to keep downtown as the center of the shopping district. Those citizens must have cherished the town they knew, bordered by Trancas on the north end and the open wetlands around the Maxwell Bridge, wetlands that housed many of the bird species we can no longer find. Few strangers ever visited and few locals ever left, a kind of Brigadoon, where the narrow roads in and out of town were rarely traveled by anyone. Perhaps in those days a quarter century ago, the Western Robin, the White Crowned Sapsucker and the Lute-Scent Warbler lingered in our fields, not yet claimed by developers.

Yellow Warbler. *Courtesy of Ray Hennessy, UnSplash.*

Soscol Avenue, late 1940s. *Courtesy of the Napa County Historical Society.*

Certainly, the wetlands were home, as they had been for thousands of years, to the Tule Wren, the Western Sandpiper, the Spoonbill Duck and the Sparrow Hawk. Birds that are endangered now by habitat destruction include the Olive-Sided Flycatcher, Cooper's and Sharp-Shinned Hawks and the Yellow Warbler.

When Professor Nelda Nocita moved to Napa to teach economics in the 1960s, fields stretched down Imola and Soscol Avenues. As a student of rural and urban history, she fought passionately against the South Napa Marketplace, understanding how it would destroy countless local businesses. She and Mike Joell collected signatures to put the South Napa development on the ballot, an initiative that was ruled invalid by the city attorney. By 1996, several big-box stores had been built on wetlands in south Napa, creating an enormous shopping development that threatened the existence of small businesses and department stores.

Ten Kinds of Snakes
Is what he remembers: finding them in
those open fields between farmhouses,
meadows and orchards where poor kids
like him could feast on nature.

Lost Nature

To the virtuous smilers of the
City Council, those fields
of imagination are now "infill."
Their joyous duty is to erect
massive concrete foundations,
housing for newcomers, on streets they'll
call "Walnut Court," though they
leveled the walnut trees first.

EPILOGUE

It's a strange feeling to be only nineteen and have nostalgia for a simpler time.
—Napa College student, 2005

Students at Napa College once learned the history of their own town. After reading about Napa of the 1950s and '60s, Montana Dudley wrote: "I worked at Vallerga's at the Redwood Plaza. Now I know why it's called store #3." She was also interested in an interview with Mary Wallis, who attended the college from 1961 to 1963. Wallis described her French teacher, Simone Fontaine: "She was very tall, and thin, and always wore floral dresses. She had the classic French red cheeks and we really liked her because she would call the guys jerks in French when they were goofing off." Montana responded: "I know the French teacher Simone Fontaine because she shops at my store. She is a sassy old lady who drives a red Mustang. I wish I could have had her as a teacher."

Other students were struck by what Jacqueline Guzman described as "the many activities kids and teenagers were able to do on the weekends. The drive-in theater, skating rink, dances at the fairgrounds. It seems so fun! Maybe that's why the morale of teenagers is different these days." Sommer Barnes commented, "One thing that I remember is when we had two bowling alleys, Bel Aire and Napa, one at each end of town." Her friend Stephanie Nicholini added: "I remember as a child going to Bel Aire Bowl Monday nights and watching my dad in his bowling league. I shop at Vallerga's and it's weird to think that my grandparents may have shopped there."

Many students lamented the loss of Brewsters. James Dennis wrote: "I remember when I was young in the eighties, going to Brewsters with my dad. We would go in there to buy the Ben Davis work shirts and boots. I was a little sad when the store closed. It was a part of my youth." Christa Burris added: "I remember shopping at Brewsters with my mom when I was little but something I didn't know was that Harris Nussbaum was a co-owner. He was a favorite teacher of mine in high school."

Christa also was interested in the stories of women's softball in the 1950s, when, under the leadership of their coach and manager, Ernie Collicutt, the Napa Shamrocks reached national prominence. Pitcher Carole Nelson established an American record in 1955. Collicutt, who headed the Bartenders, Waiters and Waitresses Union, devoted many years to promoting girls' softball, resulting in the Kiwanis Girls Softball Field on Coombs Street. Christa wrote: "I played softball for ten years in Napa, starting in the Bird Leagues as an eager eight year old, and finished out my last five years in the Kiwanis softball park on Coombs Street, playing with some of the same girls as in the third grade."

Megan Flack wrote of going to Merrill's Drugs and shopping at Brewsters:

> *I remember my grandma worked at Montgomery Wards. My aunt and I used to pick blackberries down by Embassy Suites. My dad, who is only forty-five, remembers a simpler time in Napa than I do. He remembers most of the Napa Valley being orchards and that you could walk through the orchards up to St. Helena if you wanted to. It's a strange feeling to be only nineteen and have nostalgia for a simpler time, for establishments that don't exist anymore.*

The idea that Napa had a drive-in theater fascinated Emery Meeks, while student Brian Curry, twenty years older, was able to remember "going through the drive-through restaurants such as A&W on Silverado Trail, the Foster Freeze on Lincoln and the KVON drive-in theater." Karl Poniatoski, who emigrated here as a child from Poland, commented: "It seems that people back then had a bit more fun than we do. There were a lot of interesting events in Napa, like a skating rink, two bowling alleys and a drive-in movie theater. Seems like all I ever do in Napa with my friends is nothing. It feels like Napa has gone downhill."

June Stephenson, who moved here in 1953, wrote that "Napa was the kind of town where you could go downtown on a Saturday morning and see many people you knew. Except for Woolworth's I don't remember any chain stores in the 50s or very much into the 60s. I remember when K-Mart came on Lincoln Avenue there was fear from local merchants." Chris Adams, a descendant of the Italian immigrant community, responded poignantly: "I remember the K Mart. I remember how long it used to take when we went shopping there because we would run into so many people that we knew. My mother used to say 'small world.' I haven't heard her say that for a long while."

The steep price of "progress" and the consequences of marketing the "Napa lifestyle" to outsiders are striking in these student comments. We don't listen enough to the young voices in our town; if the city fathers and mothers were listening now, it might give them pause to realize what these young people feel they have already lost. Michael Fish, who grew up in American Canyon, remarked: "The old Napa seems small and everybody who speaks gives an impression of familiarity with each other. Nowadays Napa is huge, and while you may see familiar faces, many are not." The concerns of our young people are vitally needed as we debate the changing face of our valley.

WORKS CITED

Chapter 1

Amato, Joseph. *Rethinking Home: A Case for Writing Local History*. Berkeley: University of California Press, 2002.

Anderson, Kat. *Tending the Wild: Native American Knowledge and the Management of California's Natural Resources.* Berkeley: University of California Press, 2005.

Brown, Maddie D. "General Mariano Guadalupe Vallejo and Hubert Howe Bancroft." *California Historical Quarterly*, June 1950.

Cerruti, Henry. "Ramblings in California." MSS C-E 115:2, Bancroft Library, Berkeley, 1874. Heidenreich, Linda. "Family, Race and Culture in Napa County, California." *Barksdale Essays in History*, 2000.

Combellack, Olamae. Interview with author, 2003.

Coodley, Lauren. "Green Apple." In *Napa: The Transformation of an American Town*. Charleston, SC: Arcadia, 2004.

———. "A Japanese Journey." *Napa Valley Marketplace*, 2010.

———. "What Was Said at That Table." Larry Duncan interview. *Napa Valley Marketplace*, July 2011.

Coodley, Lauren, and Paula Amen Judah. *Napa Valley Farming*. Charleston, SC: Arcadia Publishing, 2009.

Couchman, Robert. *The Sunsweet Story*. Yuba City, CA: Sunsweet Growers, 1967.

Courtney, Kevin. "Commission Wants to Preserve Von Uhlit Home." *Napa Register*, June 15, 2001.

———. "Woman Saw Town, Family Grow Together." *Napa Register*, May 6, 2003.

Donovan, Paul. "The Buildings of Lake Berryessa." Napa, CA: Napa County Historical Society, n.d.

Ezettie, Louis. "Looking into Napa's Past and Present." *Napa Register*, August 6, 1977.

Grohs, Stephanie Farrell, and Lauren Coodley. *Frankie's Journey: The Silk Road to Napa*. Sonoma, CA: Mousetail Publishing, 2014. Available through author's website, www.laurencoodley.com.

Grover, Marilyn. Correspondence with author, March 2011.

Jensen, Peter. "Napa and Solano Battled over Berryessa's Fate: Powerful Forces Aligned against Napa." *Napa Valley Register*, August 19, 2012.

Juarez-Rose, Vivian. *The Past Is Father of the Present: Spanish California*. N.p.: self-published, 1974.

Kyle, Ron. Interview with author, 2020.

Luhmann, Henry. Minutes of Farm Laborer Committee 1940s. Available at the Napa County Historical Society. Napa, California.

McKenzie, Robert. "The Monticello Rodeo and Barbeque." *Gleanings* 1, no. 4 (May 1975), Napa County Historical Society.

Menefee, C.A. *Historical Descriptive Sketch Book of Napa, Sonoma, Lake and Mendocino Counties*. Napa, CA: Reporter Publishing, 1873

Moore, John J. *The Elevator* 1, no. 27 (October 6, 1865).

Napa Daily Journal, April 14, 1918, and November 14, 1918.

Salazar, Carolyn Knief. Unpublished manuscript, September 6, 2010.

"San Francisco Boys in the Hop Fields." *Pacific Rural Press* 62, no. 9 (August 1901).

San Francisco Call, December 17, 1904. California Digital Newspaper Collection.

San Francisco Chronicle, 1923.

St. Helena Star, October 26, 1923.

Treleven, Mike. "The Prunes Are Gone, but Sunsweet Dehydrator Enjoys Second Life." *Napa Valley Register*, October 7, 2010.

Wagenknecht, John. Interview with author, 2003.

Warnock, Marilyn. Correspondence with author, 2008.

Weber, Lin. *Roots of the Present: Napa Valley 1900 to 1950*, citing *Napa Daily Journal*, February 14, 1904. St. Helena, CA: Wine Ventures Publishing, 2001.

Wheatley, David. Interview by Stephanie Grohs, 2007.

Chapter 2

Amato, Joseph. *Rethinking Home: A Case for Writing Local History*. Berkeley: University of California Press, 2002.

Brennan, Nancy, and Rita Bordwell. "This Was Napa." Napa County Historical Society (Spring 1998).

Collins, Mildred. "Home Is Where the Heart Is." *Napa Register*, June 5, 2002.

Coodley, Lauren, and Danielle Alexander. "The Army of the Immortals: Reclaiming William Jacks." *Napa Valley Marketplace*, December 2016.

Coodley, Lauren. Interview with Carol Grant, 1999.

Dong, Lorraine. Letter from Chinese Historical Society to Napa City Council. June 12, 2003.

Ericson, Greta. Oral History. St. Helena Historical Society. shstory.org.

Fisher, M.F.K. Introduction, "Napa Wine," chapter in *Silverado Squatters*, published by James Beard, 1965.

Jacks Family Scrapbook: "General Jacks has lately built a rockery in his garden on Grant Avenue which is a great curiosity in its way. Many colored stones are used in its construction, adding greatly to the effect, and on the top sits a goose through the bill of which flows a stream of water. Here and there are pots containing flowers, the whole forming a beautiful object," circa 1880s.

Jackson, Donald, ed., *The Journals of Zebulon M. Pike, with Letters and Related Documents*. Norman: University of Oklahoma, 1966.

McConahey, Meg. "Calistoga's Old Hospital Rescued from the Wrecking Ball." *Santa Rosa Press Democrat*, August 25, 2018.

Mini, Martin. *Two Families: Cavagnaro and Guisto*. Napa, CA: self-published, 1998.

Orton, Arthur. "Reconstructing the Robert Louis Stevenson 'Silverado Squatters' Cabin." N.p.: self-published, 1980.

Ryan, David. "Buyers Race to Buy New Homes at Sheveland Ranch." *Napa Valley Register*. April 4, 2005.

Sedgley, Scott. Correspondence with author, 2011.

Smith, Jane. *Napa Register*, May 22, 1973.

———. Obituary. *Napa Register*, September 14, 2006. "As a writer, she celebrated the common magic of daily life with a focus on humor and irony…Jane gave freely of herself and her writing skills for community causes such as slow growth, protection of mountain lions, the historical society and, most recently, the funding of a public pool for the community of Calistoga."

St. Helena Historical Society. https://shstory.org/research-articles.

Stevenson, Robert Louis. *A Child's Garden of Verses, 1885.* Ware, UK: Wordsworth Editions; new edition, 1994.
———. *The Silverado Squatters*. St. Helena, CA: Silverado Museum and Lewis Osborne, 1972.
Thomas, Laura. "The Real Historians." Interviews with Henry Wigger and Lou Giusto. *Late Harvest*. Ciao Productions, 1984.
Todorov, Kerana. "Ging Chan Looks Back at His People's Roots in Old Napa." *Napa Register*, August 24, 2008.
Wilson, Leonore. "The Attendant Trails." In *Tremendum, Augustum*. American Fork, UT: Aldrich Press, 2014.
Yount, George. *George C. Yount and His Chronicles of the West: Comprising Extracts from the Memoirs and from the Orange Clark Narrative*. Denver, CO: Old West Publishing, 1996.

Chapter 3

Almstrom, Margaret. Interview with author, 2003.
Bordwell, Rita. "History of the Napa Fire Department from 1859 to 1962." Available at the Napa County Historical Society.
———. "Napa County Labor Movement was Born of Depression." *Napa Register*, March 30, 1963.
———. Obituary. *Napa Register*, February 22, 1975.
Brambila, Maria. Correspondence with author, 2003.
Bray, Carol. "Napa Firefighters Cookbook" edited by and illustrated by Richard Rains, available at Napa County Historical Society.
Brennan, Nancy. "This Was Napa." Napa County Historical Society, Spring 1998.
Bryant, Dorothy. *Confessions of Madame Psyche*. Introduction by J.J. Wilson. New York: Feminist Press, 1998.
Campbell, Mary. Letter to author, February 8, 2009.
Coodley, Lauren. *Napa: The Transformation of an American Town*. Arcadia, 2004.
———. "Researching Rita Bordwell." *Napa Valley Marketplace,* 2007.
———. "Shrimp Boat" *The Same River Twice*. Crockett, CA: Sugartown Publishing, 2018.
Coodley, Lauren, and Danielle Alexander. "The Sight of 27 Grown Men Cooking Their Own Meals." *Napa Valley Marketplace*, January 2018.
Coodley, Lauren, with Stephanie Grohs. "Your World for a Moment: The Recovered History of Carl Franco." *Napa Valley Marketplace*, October 2015.
Courtney, Kevin, "Napa Pipe Plant Loads Its Final Railcar." *Napa Register*, September 30, 2005.

———. "Napa Steelworkers Tell Their Stories." *Napa Register*, September 30, 2005.

———. "Rough Rider Building Razed for Flood Control." *Napa Valley Register*, August 2002.

Edington, Astrid. "Firefighters Honor 'Napa's Great Lady.'" *Napa Register*, October 4, 1969.

Faux, Jeff. *The Global Class War: How America's Bipartisan Elite Lost Our Future—and What It Will Take to Win It Back*. Hoboken, NJ: John Wiley & Sons, 2006.

Franco, Carl. Obituary. *The Garment Worker* (Journal of the United Garment Workers of America), April 5, 1946.

Johnson, Jeff. "Growing Up in Napa on West Lincoln Avenue." *Napa Valley Marketplace Magazine*. Archived at Napa County Historical Society, September 2016.

Kammen, Carol. *On Doing Local History*. Lanham, MD: Altamira Press, 2001.

King, Phyllis. "About This Fourth Estate." Unpublished, July 22, 1955.

Lund, John. "Historical Impacts of Geothermal Resources on the People of North America." Proceedings of World Geothermal Congress, Florence, Italy, October 1995.

Manasse, Peter. Letter to author, 2006.

McKee, Brent. Correspondence with author, April 2020.

Menefee, C.A. *Historical and Descriptive Sketch Book of Napa, Solano, and Lake Counties.* Reporter Publishing Company, 1873.

Napa County Reporter, April 6, 1872, January 15, 1886, May 21, 1892.

Napa Daily Journal, July 3, 1875.

Napa Journal. "Building, Roads Built Here By WPA." August 1, 1941.

———. "Las Posadas Camp Reopened by S.R.A." December 23, 1936.

———. "WPA Accomplishments in Napa County Described in Report by Area Manager." October 18, 1940.

Napa Register, February 19, 1895, July 18, 1897.

Nelson, Barry. Correspondence with author, 2020.

Prestinary, Patricia. *Napa State Hospital*. Charleston, SC: Arcadia, 2014. Correspondence from Cindy Hummer and Peter Zwetsloot.

Reyna, Liz. Unpublished manuscript, 2009.

Santa Rosa Republican. "Napa WPA Project." July 11, 1939.

Smith, Jane. *Napa Register*, May 22, 1973.

St. Helena Star. "Camp Site at Los Posados." October 27, 1933.

———. "Forestry Here: Its Story..." April 2, 1959.

Swett, Ira, and Harry Aitken. *The Napa Valley Route*. Glendale, CA: Interurbans, 1975.

Vu, Dr. Phong. Correspondence with author, October 2009.

Weber, Lin. *Old Napa Valley History to 1900*. Wine Ventures Publishing, 1998.

———. *Roots of the Present: Napa Valley 1900 to 1950*. St. Helena, CA: Wine Ventures Publishing, 2001.

Chapter 4

Aaron, Peggy. Correspondence with author, 2020.

Amen, Michael. *The Dream Bowl: Where Goodman, Ellington, and the Grateful Dead Convene.* Boulder, CO: Westview, 2019.

Aultman, Chris. Correspondence with author, 2003.

Brown, S.L. *Play: How It Shapes the Brain, Opens the Imagination, and Invigorates the Soul*. New York: Avery Penguin Press, 2009.

Clerici, Andrew. Letter to author, 2005.

Coodley, Lauren. "I Danced." In *The Same River Twice*. Crockett, CA: Sugartown Press, 2018.

Deyerle, Michael. "A Trip Down Memory 'Lanes.'" *Napa Valley Register,* December 12, 2020.

Dreessen, Kathleen. "Simply Putt, Paradise Miniature Golf Offers Great Entertainment." *Napa Valley Register,* April 24, 2005.

Fogerty, Deanna. Correspondence with author, 2020.

Ford, Jim. "Napa As It Was: Mobile Dating." *Napa Valley Register*, December 6, 2010.

Harrison, Judy. Correspondence with author, 2020.

Hill, John. "The Hatt Building." *Explore Napa*. https://explorenapa.org.

Hurley, Marlene Wilson. Correspondence with author, 2020.

Jobe, Ellwin. Correspondence with author, 2020.

Judah, Paula Amen. Excerpt from "Hoffman Avenue." In *Añoraza*. McKinleyville, CA: Fithian Press, 2016.

Longoria, Terry. Correspondence with author, 2020.

Malloy, Thomas. Interview with author, 2003.

Manasse, Peter. Letter to author, 2006.

Mathews, Cathy. Correspondence with author, 2003 and 2020.

McKee, Brent. Correspondence with author, 2020. Living New Deal. https://livingnewdeal.org.

Mini, Martin. *Two Families: Cavagnaro and Guisto*. Napa, CA: Self-published, 1998.

Murray, Doug. Correspondence with author, 2020.

Napa Journal. "New Director for Recreation Work Comes Here Monday." January 25, 1941.

———. "Tourney Winners Get Certificates." April 2, 1941.

Napa Register, February 13, 1885.

Smith, Jane. *Napa Register,* June 27, 1994.

Stanley, Pat. "More Memory Lane." *Napa Valley Register*, April 6, 2003, including quote from Rhonda Torres.

Vu, Dr. Phong. Correspondence with author, 2003 and October 2009.

Yerger, Rebecca. "The Movie Man." *Napa Register*, March 23, 2001.

Chapter 5

Baird, Bruce. "Napa Woolworth's Closing in January." *Napa Register*, October 14, 1994.

Barnhill, Bonnie Lee. "Around the Grapevine." *UFCW Newsletter*, August 1981.

Brennan, Nancy. "Mary Ann Doud in This Was Napa." Napa County Historical Society. Spring, 1998.

———. *Napa County Record*, July 2, 1992.

Coodley, Lauren. "When They Sold the Union Market." In *The Same River Twice*. Crockett, CA: Sugartown Press, 2018.

Coodley, Lauren. "Golden Carrot." In *The Same River Twice*. Crockett, CA: Sugartown Press, 2018.

Courtney, Kevin. "Clock Tower Toppling Set for Sunday." *Napa Register*, January 31, 2001.

———. "Doctor's Orders: Larry Must Quit," *Napa Register*, December 9, 1998.

———. "Mom-and-Pop Stores Losing, Moving out of Downtown." *Napa Register*, February 22, 2004.

Dietiker-Yolo, Linda. Letter from Commission on the Status of Women. May 26, 1981.

Duarte, Jesse. "St. Helena's Greta Ericson Looks Back on an Eventful Life." *St. Helena Star*, July 26, 2016.

Ericson, Greta. Oral History. shstory.org. Greta concluded "What else can I say. I love the town. I've been a member of the Soroptimist Club here for 35 years and was Citizen of the Year in 2000, and I appreciated it very much so I'll just live and die right here." She passed away in July 2020.

Ezettie, Louis. Articles, June-September 1961. Courtesy of Napa County Historical Society.

Ford, Jim. "Napa's Department Stores in World War II." *Napa Register*, December 3, 2004.

Friedman, Rachel. Interview by Lauren Coodley, 2003.

Gracia, Roxanne. Correspondence with author, 2020.

Gracia, Tom. Obituary. *Napa Register*, August 9, 2016. "He graduated from University of Iowa, where he met the love of his life, Roxann Gracia (Miller). They were married on October 1, 1977 and settled in the quiet little town of Napa. Tom began work as a Pharmacist at Family Drug and became the heart and soul of the business for 40 years. He was a caring, old fashioned pharmacist, who knew everyone's parents, kids, grandparents, and grandkids and answered the inevitable question, "Hey Tom, what do you think about..."

Guadagni, Ray. *The Adventures of the Squeezebox Kid.* Raymond A. Guadagni, 2016.

Huffman, Jennifer. "Giovannoni Still Filling Food Sacks after All These Years." *Napa Register*, October 2, 2011.

Kammen, Carol. *On Doing Local History*. Lanham, MD: Altamira Press, 2003.

Langer, Patty. Interview with author, 2003.

Mathews, Cathy. Interview with author, 2003.

McFee, Michael. "Service Is Our Business" in *Shinemaster*. Pittsburgh, PA: Carnegie Mellon University Press, 2006. Used with permission.

Mini, Martin. *Two Families: Cavagnaro and Guisto*. Napa, CA: self-published, 1998.

Munk, Ken. Correspondence with author, 2010.

Poirier, Juliane. "Napa Health Food Store Closing Doors After 29 Years: Owner Lorna Birdsall Planning for Next Phase of Life." *Napa Valley Register*, March 25, 2014

Pollock, Sudie. Correspondence with author, 2020.

Schwartz, Harvey. Correspondence with author, 2020.

Stanley, Pat. "After 28 Years, Napan Decides to Hang It Up." *Napa Register*, May 20, 2006.

Stephenson, June. Letter to author, 2003.

Weber, Lin. *Under the Vine and the Fig Tree*. St. Helena: Wine Ventures Publishing, 2003

Wyman, Alisha. "Nor-Mar, Napa's Philanthropic Store, to Close: Fabric Shop Funded 14 Students in College." *Napa Valley Register*, March 16, 2014.

Yerger, Rebecca. "Celebrating the Sweet Life of the Candy Making Bryant Family." *Napa Register*, May 13, 2001.

Chapter 6

Amato, Joseph. *Rethinking Home: A Case for Writing Local History*. Berkeley: University of California Press, 2002.

Baldwin, Bruce, Douglas Goldman, David J. Keil and Robert Patterson. *The Jepson Manual*. Berkeley: University of California Press, 2012.

Bartlett, W.P. *More Happenings in California: A Series of Sketches of the Great California Outdoors*. Boston: Christopher Publishing, 1928.

Berner, Murray, Bill Grummer, Robin Leong and Mike Rippey. *Breeding Birds of Napa*. Napa Solano Audubon Society. Napa, California.

Coodley, Lauren. "The Flight of Feathers: Researching Birds in Napa." Includes letter from Elmer Bickford. *Napa Valley Marketplace*, January 2006.

———. "Ten Kinds of Snakes." In *The Same River Twice*. Crockett, CA: Sugartown Press, 2018.

Coodley, Lauren, with Stephanie Grohs. "Your World for a Moment: The Recovered History of Carl Franco." *Napa Valley Marketplace*, October 2015.

Grossinger, Robin. *Napa Valley Historical Ecology Atlas: Exploring a Hidden Landscape of Transformation and Resilience*. Berkeley: University of California Press, 2012

Johnson, Jeff. "Growing Up in Napa on West Lincoln Avenue." *Napa Valley Marketplace Magazine* (September 2016). Archived at Napa County Historical Society, Napa, California.

Manfree, Amber. Correspondence with author, 2020.

Minnich, R.A. *California's Fading Wildflowers: Lost Legacy and Biological Invasions.* Berkeley: University of California Press, 2008.

Murray, Doug. Correspondence with author, 2020.

Norris, Tony. Correspondence with author, 2020.

Schwartz, Harvey. Correspondence with author, 2020.

Stephenson, June. Correspondence with author, 2003.

Sugino, Nobuo. "Pressed Flower Craft." Prezi.com. http://www.pressed-flowercraft.com/histperspect.html.

Verardo, Denzel. *Napa Valley from Golden Fields to Purple Harvest*. Napa, CA: Napa Historical Society, 1986.

Epilogue

Coodley, Lauren. "Napa College Reflects on Napa History." *Napa Valley Marketplace*, June 2005.

ABOUT THE AUTHOR

Lauren Coodley began her career tutoring students for the GED and teaching night school psychology at Napa's junior college in the late 1970s. She invented and taught classes ranging from American women's history to overcoming math anxiety to Napa-Vallejo history. She was the first tenured woman to teach history. Since her retirement, she has been caring for her grandsons and continuing her writing career.

Her books include: *Napa: The Transformation of an American Town* (Arcadia, 2004); *The Land of Orange Groves and Jails: Upton Sinclair's California* (Heyday Press, 2004); *California: A Multicultural Documentary History* (Pearson, 2008); *Napa Valley Farming* (Arcadia Publishing, 2009), co-author Paula Amen Judah; *Napa Valley Chronicles* (The History Press, 2013); *Upton Sinclair: California Socialist Celebrity Intellectual* (University of Nebraska, 2013); *Frankie's Journey: The Silk Road to Napa* (Mousetail Press, 2015), co-author Stephanie Grohs; and *The Same River Twice* (Sugarland Press, 2018).